West By Sea

Michelle Marie Boullianne Beale
Edward Kenneth Beale

West By Sea is a work of nonfiction. Some names and identifying details have been changed.

Printed in the United States of America on acid-free paper.

www.westbysea.com

9 8 7 6 5 4 3 2 1

FIRST EDITION

Photos © Edward K. Beale and Michelle M. B. Beale
or used with permission.

Book design by Edward K. Beale. Edited by Alison Downs.

Published in the United States of America.

Library of Congress Control Number: 2016901529
Self Published by Expeditionaire, Mystic, Connecticut.
Beale, Edward
West by sea: a treasure hunt that spans the globe / Edward Beale.

ISBN: 978-0692383100
1. Nonfiction / Travel 2. Nonfiction / Cancer
16.02.16

For our family and friends

The world is a book,
and those who do not travel
read only a page.

~ *Saint Augustine*

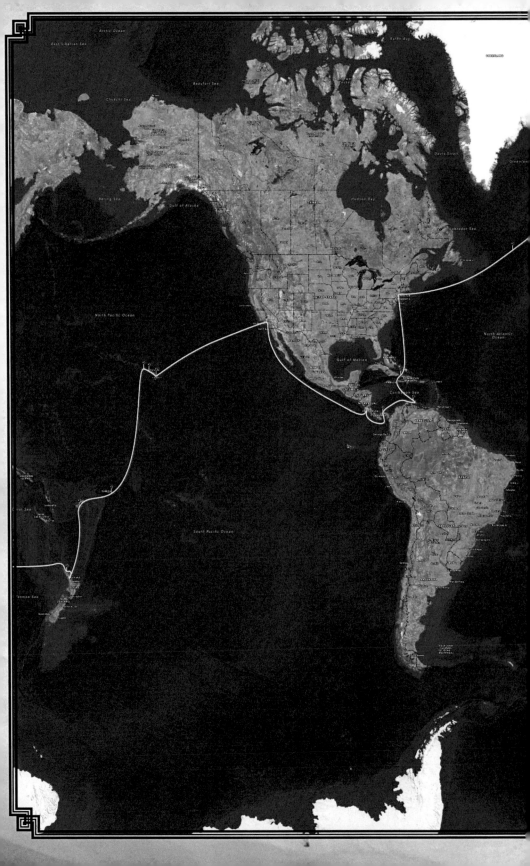

The credit belongs to the person who is actually
in the arena; who strives valiantly; who errs,
who comes short again and again; but who does
actually strive to do the deeds; who knows great
enthusiasms, the great devotions; who spends
herself in a worthy cause; who at the best
knows in the end the triumph of high achievement,
and who at the worst, if she fails, at least fails
while daring greatly, so that her place shall never
be with those cold and timid souls who neither
know victory nor defeat.

~ US President Theodore Roosevelt

PROLOGUE

In the late spring of 1999, we flew the supersonic transport *Concorde* to Paris. It was our honeymoon, and for two aviation fanatics it was a dream come true. Three days in the city of light, then the Chunnel by Eurostar for three days in London, followed by a six day transatlantic crossing aboard Queen Elizabeth II, and we were hopelessly hooked. Our suitcases were just one trip young, but we already wanted more.

Early in our marriage we decided to shun gifts and give each other the gift of travel experiences instead. So it was only natural to dream about giving each other the world, a full circumnavigation. We watched friends set out on their own world journeys. Some did it on a shoestring, the proverbial "backpacking around the world" approach. Some did it by air, touching down for a week or so, then onward to find the next time zone. There are so many ways to circle the globe, and no shortage of travel and adventure outfitters willing to craft the experience. So we knew it would happen, someday. And then Michelle's cancer changed everything.

When we thought back to our honeymoon, round trip by ship seemed to be just the thing. There are many benefits to traveling this way. You unpack once and can then enjoy a floating oasis of calm in the middle of a chaotic journey. You wake up every morning in the same place, and yet a new place, with new things to see, people to meet, and currencies to spend. The food may not always be great, but it typically arrives hot and in large portions. There may not always be sunshine, but there is always hot coffee.

A journey around the world cannot be undertaken on a whim. It requires months, if not years of planning. Between Ed's 14 deployments and four expeditions to the poles, and Michelle's extensive operational planning background, we had the expertise to pull it off. We saved our pennies for 15 years, then watched the ebb and flow of life for the perfect chance to cross the gangway and go. The window opened in the summer of 2013, and we structured our lives to allow us to be gone for half the year. We decided to view the experience as "living abroad." We did not know just how accurate that would be.

So what is it like to be stuck on a ship full of Aussies, Kiwis, and the occasional Brit or Yank, then travel across 6 continents, through 40 ports in 28 countries, and sail 34,634 nautical miles in 105 days, in the face of a lifechanging illness? That, dear reader, is what you are about to discover.

For you, we wanted to craft a book unlike anything you have ever seen before. We hope you enjoy this adventure around the world, and that our story inspires you to travel well and far, and do amazing things.

Get out there, get moving, and outdistance the impossible.

~ Michelle and Edward

Sailing
Segment
One

Throughout the centuries there were those who took first steps, down new roads, armed with nothing but their own vision. ~ Ayn Rand

7

The drama, anticipation, and tears are over. This morning Ed and I begin a journey around the world. As I make final preparations to meet the ship, the sky is warm and mercifully rainless. Our Australian friends Merrilyn and John have spent the past week showing us lesser-known attractions around Sydney, including the 1770 landing site of Captain Cook in Botany Bay. I will always remember sneaking into the Australian rules football (footie) match between the Sydney Swans and Fremantle, and still regret the final score was a 70-70 tie. No singing.

A short drive to the White Bay terminal in Rozelle just west of downtown brings me to the ship. Limited space means limited gear, just what we passengers can carry. The large luggage is carefully tagged, marked with our names and stateroom number. A loading crew spirits it away, I am told, to the cabin. Ed and I step aboard what will be our home for the next four months, a floating oasis on a planet of water.

Four of the five bags are waiting after I clear customs, the mug shot photographer, and x-ray security checkpoint. My assigned cabin steward Bonie (pronounced "bone-ee") tracks down the fifth bag, and I can finally relax. The initial preparations are complete. Anything more I might need will have to be found along the way. I am settled in and ready to start one hundred and five days of adventure.

The ship is moored "port side to" and bow out. With the tide behind we spring away from the berth under pilot, shadowed by three yellow and green harbor tugs. All lines are clear in the final minutes of daylight, and we join the busy harbor traffic just west of the famous Sydney Harbor Bridge.

An orange and pink sunset illuminates our wake for a few brief moments. Then night drops its velvet curtain to plunge the decks into darkness. As we round the North Head sanctuary and turn into a moonless black, ripples become long swells that rock me to sleep.

Daily Position: S 33º 52', E 151º 11'
Status: In Port, Sydney, Australia
Weather: clear, 18ºC, wind W 15 kts, 1 m waves

DAY 1

SYDNEY, AUSTRALIA

MAY 20

DAY 2

GREAT BARRIER REEF

MAY 21

With the East Australia Current behind us, we cover more than 300 miles by sunup. The first night aboard ship is always hard, like trying to bed down inside a washing machine. The sounds are unfamiliar, the mattress is not your own, and everything moves. It is not a rocking motion, at least not always, but more a lilting, drunken wedding dance with you at the center and shoved by the guests - first left, then back, then up, then right-forward-down and the cycle repeats with unpredictable irregularity. By morning I have fresh bruises.

Ed and I greet the sun with a walk about the main weather deck, and spy a dolphin pod converging from the starboard quarter. Soon the rail is lined with other passengers hoping for a glimpse. We smile politely and trade morning pleasantries, but we remain strangers. There will be time to share stories, but watching dolphins at sea is a rare treat not to be interrupted with small talk. Pairs and singles gambol in the swirling surf kicked up by our twin screws, fins flashing in the spray.

The first full day underway also means exploring. I find the galley and am happy to discover coffee and deep mugs. Tea and coffee at all hours is expected and a sign of a well-mannered ship. My ship does not disappoint. Breakfast: a croissant, fresh cantelope, blueberries, watermelon, coffee, and my morning vitamins and medication. The salt air is probably to blame for my appetite. Later, I commandeer a burlwood table in the small ship's library to catch up on news from home, and Ed finds an open deck chair on the leeward side to update the travel journal.

At the evening meal we dine with Maxine and Bruce from Melbourne. They too are making the full journey around the world, and today are celebrating Maxine's birthday. Then, completely exhausted from a day packed with discovery, I turn in early and dream of a bed that does not move.

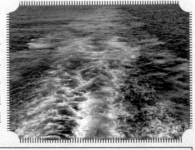

Everything we hear is an opinion, not a fact. Everything we see is a perspective, not the truth. ~ Marcus Aurelius

Travel is about the gorgeous feeling of teetering in the unknown.
" Gaby Basora

5

Up early and at the pilot station by 5:30 a.m. for a dark transit in to port. A quick sunrise reveals high overcast and dark, threatening clouds. The locals consider this strange for normally sunny Brisbane. At breakfast I meet a Kiwi couple. The husband is a self-described displaced "limey" and asks if I know the origin of the expression.

In the rush to get to sea, you always forget *something* ashore. I am no different, and so shopping is on the agenda. A 15-minute shuttle ride brings me to the heart of downtown, festooned with jagged metal murals and a patchwork of modern and historic storefronts.

With last minute purchases in hand, Ed and I make our way down to the Brisbane River, dodging puddles. The Royal Historical Society of Queensland maintains an early cultural heritage museum in a three-story stone building with bars on the windows, constructed by convict labor. It served as the prison's storehouse, and the bars kept convicts *out*. At first, the area was exclusively a prison. Lifting the settlement ban brought free immigrants from the 50 mile perimeter to the city center. The museum's collection boasts the original workbench of Andrew Petrie, the first free tradesman in Brisbane. He fixed the windmill and started a dynasty of carpenters. Artifacts on display from the early- and mid-20th century waves of Italian colonization include the first espresso machine on the continent, which helped establish the northeast Australian coffee culture.

Looking for lunch, I spot the quirky Pancake Manor housed inside an old church. The tuxedoed staff serve mushroom crepes with sundried tomato sauce, salad, and coffee in glass mugs. Around the corner, first editions and one million tomes on the uneven shelves of Archives Fine Books claim my last happy hours in Oz, wandering the aisles. Tonight we begin eight continuous days at sea enroute to Singapore, chasing the sunset.

Daily Position: S 27º 28' 05" E 153º 01' 40"
Status: In Port, starboard side to
Weather: overcast & rainy, 17º C, light airs, 0 m waves

Daily Position: S 22º 11' 03" E 151º 10' 18"
Status: underway in the Capricorn Channel, heading 313º
Weather: alto stratus, 22º C, wind SW 21 kts, 1 m waves

DAY 4

CORAL SEA

MAY 23

E arly in our marriage my husband and I made a commitment to each other: to purchase experiences before we purchased things. We started our honeymoon with a supersonic flight and three days in Paris, a Chunnel ride and three days in London, then a Transatlantic return cruise to New York City. For us, travel is not an option: it is an imperative. It is what it means to be *us*.

Some people choose to travel less and collect more - automobiles, houses, clothing, toys, or jewelry. Life is about setting priorities in the face of scarcity. We made a deliberate choice, to exchange time and money for memories made together at the ends of the earth. The decision to drop everything and point our footsteps around the world was easy. But getting to this day spent offshore and tracking the Great Barrier Reef was not. Not by a long shot.

O n the way to Cabin D614 aboard Sea Princess, Ed and I shipped our possessions to long-term storage. There is no good way to describe the experience of watching all your worldly "stuff" disappear in a truck driven away by strangers. Surreal, maybe. I might never see any of that stuff again. Here at sea, I wonder if any of it is that important.

We listed the house for sale. Having no mortgage payment would have helped with trip expenses, but the market was still bad and the house had not sold before we left to meet the ship. We pre-signed papers to conduct a closing at any time during the voyage, from any point on the globe. Ed's parents will help coordinate any on-site issues with the property itself. And what to do with the cat? She will spend the summer with my parents. Who will make a bigger sacrifice, I wonder - Mom and Dad, or LaVache? Will any of them ever forgive me? Maybe it is time I asked, "Why am I doing this again?"

By the fourth day of the journey and still pinching myself, this is still real. I have done it. Six months of sacrifice and pain are behind me. Hang on now - this is only getting started.

If you can dream it you can do it.
~ Walt Disney

At the age of 36, I was diagnosed with brain cancer. Six days later I underwent a craniotomy to resect a tumor the size of a small lemon. In the months leading up to an almost casually ordered magnetic resonance imaging procedure, the Hurricane Katrina disaster and its aftermath in New Orleans and Mississippi had consumed my every waking hour. At the time I was the volunteer advocate for over 300 military families at a major Coast Guard base on the U. S. Gulf Coast. My focus was on their needs. I thought my debilitating headaches were caused by the stress of long hours spent in disaster relief. Instead, preposterously, it was "Fifi the Fiend." After the surgery and years spent in a haze of daily pain, I felt like someone had flipped a switch and I had *myself* back again. But the battle had just begun.

The tumor was a grade two oligodendroglioma, a cancer of the connective tissue surrounding neurons in the brain. Just eleven months later, I had a second surgery to further debulk the site. Updated pathology showed the tumor had become a grade two oligoastrocytoma. My doctors took a wait-and-see approach, but my symptoms intensified. Images from 2009 showed "Fifi" was growing. I aggressively researched experimental treatments, and was accepted for a clinical trial at Boston's Massachusetts General Hospital. The trial involved 30 days of precisely targeted high-energy proton radiation. This procedure confined the effects to within one millimeter of the tumor, and carefully avoided healthy tissue. During the last week of radiation I celebrated a "Made it to 40" party with family and friends.

Almost four years later, with a positive checkup and a smile, my doctors cleared me to take this adventure of a lifetime. I was determined to make the trip, and by my example, inspire all of you to attack your dreams, to live your lives with urgency. In the next one hundred dred pages, the battle continues.

Daily Position: S 16º 37' 22" E 145º 46' 31"
Status: passing Endeavour Reef, rounding Cape Flattery
Weather: overcast, 24º C, wind SE 27 kts, 3 m waves

Daily Position: S 10º 33' 51" E 142º 05' 38"
Status: Westerly course across the Gulf of Carpentaria
Weather: partly cloudy, 28º C, wind SE 25 kts, 3m waves

DAY 6

Morning at sea assaults the senses. Your first conscious thought is very often "I am still here and the place is still moving." It has been said that when traveling, your soul follows twenty four hours in your wake. But ever onward is the way of ships, and you stumble topside each morning in a new place. With your soul a day behind, you have no choice - you must always start fresh.

Light reflected from wavelets through the porthole gives clues about the weather, but it is the smell that compels you to leave the warm cocoon of your rack (bed) and get moving. The aroma of breakfast wafts up from the galley (kitchen), vaporized grease in the vents mixing with the scents of coffee percolating and fresh baking bread. The glorious Pavlovian fragrance is also a cruel joke. In the early morning quest for sustenance and caffeine, a treck to the galley requires crossing the weather decks. There are perils above, and critical choices to be made before moving.

CORAL SEA

When poking your head topside, will you pick the leeward or windward side - a coin flip that is usually wrong? Will puddles in the scuppers drench your topsiders and rain spatter your face? Or will a fair salty breeze lift your mood? Should you don the rough woolly watch cap and snug parka, or leather flip-flops and tinted sunglasses? Hunger beckons and sleep is gone. Resigned to your fate, you place bare feet on chilly deck plates to be shocked suddenly and fully awake. And so the day begins.

Like most days, Ed is up and about first. The winter sky is still dark, the air moisture-heavy and the decks still wet from the daily wash down. Dodging sailboats, we put the bow solidly to the west, round Australia's northeast tip, and disembark the Great Barrier Reef pilot to a sturdy yellow boat from Booby Island.

MAY 25

Five passengers also take the boat, accompanying one of their mates who has fallen ill. Free of the ship, they will stop moving long enough to be caught by their uncoupled souls. Slowly waving goodbye, I continue into my own fresh tomorrows, pressing west.

Being in a ship is being in a jail, with the chance of being drowned.
~ Samuel Johnson

The secret to your future is hidden in your daily routine.
~ Mike Murdock

The first week has passed and for the first time I find myself among familiar faces. Yesterday's strangers are suddenly today's old friends. With so much to process, there has been little time for routine. But routine is absolutely essential to sanity when the days underway mount one upon another with monotonous regularity, the passing of dark islands and distant ships the only punctuation in an otherwise soporific run-on sentence. By the first Sunday I have a routine for waking, for washing, for breaking fast, for exercise, for study, for music, for dinner, drinks, relaxation and sleep. I have regular tablemates for the evening meal and am on a first name basis with many members of the crew. When walking the decks, I angle left to pass like a good Australian. And I am quickly running out of clean socks.

oon reports is a nautical tradition. On a clear day, the Navigator or Captain sights the sun at its peak, and announces noon with eight bells. Combined with a precise chronometer, the noon sun line is an easy way to calculate longitude, and reckon accurate distance sailed east or west. On modern ships, *noon reports* is a time for the bridge crew to update all on board, with the daily distance "made good," the forecast weather, and our planned overnight track. Many days the Captain himself does the honors, and often throws in a slightly off-color nautical joke or bit of seafaring trivia.

At supper I dress up a bit to end the week. My tablemates Karen and Roger are marking their anniversary. The cooks bring over a small celebratory cake with lit candle (an open flame at sea being a very rare sight indeed). Special events away from home can be bittersweet. Still, they generously share a small slice of the deliciously decadent chocolate explosion draped in dark ganache. Skipping through the islands of Indonesia spread out like a smile, I am sustained by new routines decorated by sweetness and light.

Daily Position: S 9º 29' 38", E 133º 37' 21"
Status: 19 kts, West-north-westerly across the Arafura Sea
Weather: overcast showers, 27º C, wind E 30 kts, 2m waves

Daily Position: S 8º 31' 48" E 127º 45' 45"
Status: 19 kts, Palau Leti to starboard, East Timor to port
Weather: overcast, 27º C, wind S 19 kts, 2m waves

DAY 8

ARAFURA SEA

MAY 27

Yawning but awake, I am up early to walk about the decks. It is overcast, hot, and humid. This is not so much a change as it is a sudden and sobering slap in the face, a blast furnace of moisture impossible to ignore. Normally the change to summer takes weeks and months, but it has happened in mere days. After Saturday's turn, we now parallel the equator and make less than 100 nautical miles of "northing" each day. But in the tropics, latitude does not really matter. It is always summer and lots of it.

Heading below after a quick scrounge for breakfast, I begin *the great laundry search*. The ship has very limited coin-operated machines, and aboard a ship full of passengers, each with a week's worth of laundry, competition for machines is frenzied and fierce. I get access to a machine right away. Ed split loads between machines three decks apart, and gets plenty of exercise running between them. The wash cycle runs for twenty five minutes but the dry cycles are "longer," making dryers the choke points of the operation.

Sadly, the dryers are also quite ineffective. So later in the day my cabin is strewn with bits of clothing hanging from every horizontal surface, rail and hook. I string a bungee clothesline with preinstalled hooks between the door handle of the head (bathroom) and one of the lockers (closets). I get good practice for the limbo as I come and go during the rest of the day, ducking under t-shirts.

Escaping the laundry rooms at last, I attend a short lecture about navigating the ship, given by one of the third officers. Getting a peek behind the curtain is time well spent. In addition to basic chart work, he discusses ships position keeping, propulsion systems, hull contour and watch structure. Navigation of any vessel on the oceans of the world is an intricate and demanding endeavor. Position be damned: right now I would probably trade all that sophisticated gear for a working dryer.

If I don't do laundry today, I'm gonna have to buy new clothes tomorrow. ~ Anna Paquin

A t breakfast we meet a returned soldier, an Australian Army Captain from World War II named Stanley Bradley. He is 93-years-young and one of those rare people with no regrets and a dense treasure trove of tales, both tall and true. The right key will unleash them. He will celebrate his 94th birthday while aboard ship, and would be going all the way around if not for his doctor's orders to return to Australia every 90 days. A dream thwarted by bureaucracy, and yes he is bitter.

Stan waves us over and we sit enthralled for the next three hours. He tells of wartime wounds, campaigns throughout Southeast Asia, and (as the only member of his unit to speak any Japanese) of walking alone into an enemy camp to accept their surrender in 1945. After everything he'd survived, he thought that day "was it." With pride he regales us of pioneering underwater gear with Jacques Cousteau, his son's commercial diving outfit (the third largest in the world), and about his darling wife. She succumbed to dementia twelve years ago, and he sheds tears of love in memory of their 58 years together.

D uring the afternoon the ship passes north of Pulau Sangeang in the Flores Sea, a perfect cone that squeezes heavy moisture into puffy white clouds. The ship has been moving through the calm tropical waters at close to 20 knots. We have successfully skirted the afternoon thunderheads for days, and today is no exception.

In the evening Ed and I stroll the decks to work off dinner. As we get closer to the Equator the temperature hardly fluctuates, leaving each moment almost exactly like the last. Still, the sunsets arrive in brilliant regalia, the fiery colors above in stark contrast to the inky and placid ocean below.

Photography at night is almost impossible from the deck of a moving ship, but I could not leave the Southern Hemisphere without trying to capture the famous Southern Cross. Onward we sail, with hope for a fine morning.

DAY 9 · ARAFURA SEA · MAY 28

Daily Position: S 7º 50' 39", E 118º 56' 03"
Status: Underway 20 knots, abeam Lesser Sunda Islands
Weather: overcast, 29º C, S 10 kts, flat calm seas

Daily Position: S 5º 06' 54" E 112º 08' 24"
Status: Underway in the Banda Sea
Weather: scattered cumulus, 30º C, NW 10 kts, sea calm

DAY 10

Flat calm overnight. In the sweltering heat, and with no ship motion to move air about the cabin, I toss and turn all night. Unable to sleep, I decide to dress and go up on deck, with camera in hand. I step topside to greet the grand mistress of all sunrises. The unbroken surface of the water barely ripples, oily-like and tranquil, pressed down by tropical heat. On the starboard quarter a full fireworks show of boiling blues and raging reds bubbles out to clutch at our little floating speck. With a blink and a tease a single orange ray twinkles through the distant overcast, dragging more friends aloft until the full promise of morning is fulfilled with flame. Sights like this last mere minutes, and today I am lucky to be here, an unexpected interloper in a magical domain.

A ship's daily routine does not stop, even for special sunrises. It has been over a week with no rain. The deck crew is hard at work with hose and bucket and brush, clearing the scuppers of accumulated salt and grime with a fresh water washdown.

BANDA SEA

With the clock regression overnight we are now a full twelve hours off from home. It feels strange to find myself a world apart. Even with the time conversion made easy, there is no easy way to get home from here. I am on the downside of the planet, unable to go farther without starting back again.

In the late morning I attend a briefing about our upcoming port calls, grab a hasty brunch, then walk the decks for exercise accompanied by the islands of Indonesia. The sea is now barely textured by a light westerly breeze on the bow. Back at my cabin, I discover my passport returned by the ship's immigration representative, containing proper landing cards for Singapore and Malaysia.

MAY 29

The chef prepares lobster for tonight's special "candlelight dinner." There is a real aversion to open flames at sea, however. The meal comes with lowered galley lighting - and no candles.

> *The things you own end up owning you.*
> *~ Tyler Durden*

> *The mind is everything. What you think is what you become.*
> *~ Buddha*

Selat Karimata Strait separates Borneo on our starboard side and Sumatra on our port as the day dawns bright and blistering.

Today I feel like I am coming down with a cold, and I hope Ed does not catch it. It is influenza season in Australia and perhaps one of the other passengers came aboard with the sniffles or worse. By the afternoon it is time to visit the ship's small clinic and the medical officer for antibiotics. Apart from a daily battle with brain cancer, there is not much worse than being ill at sea. I am especially disappointed too, because the day is of great importance, and this time I will only watch.

Since the dawn of history, the *rite of passage* ceremony helped forge strong team bonds around a shared experience. Out upon the waters, the daily sameness can lull an unwary swab or pollywog into a false sense of security, a lack of trepidation unwise in the face of possibilities wielded by the unknown. This is precisely why from time to time the old salts must visit and offer tribute at the royal and watery court. The briny deep holds many treacherous secrets, and those secrets must be respected. For the cavalier, arrogance can be deadly. Or worse.

Lo! It is the line that calls, the elusive line that girds the planet, the invisible Equator. Only through careful inspection and arduous trials will a vessel be granted passage between hemispheres. The call goes out to all pollywogs: King Neptune commands your attendance at the equatorial trials of our good ship, where he will pass sentence on the accused!

Charges must be read and answered, funny bones excised, the great ship's Captain must be tossed into the drink, and the fish - yes the dreaded fish - must be kissed. Now, let the sludging begin.

The right of passage is now complete. All ye Shellbacks old and new, be it known: the ship's company has been found worthy. Yonder line marks the top of the planet, so voyage on!

Daily Position: S 1º 15' 37", E 107º 36' 54"
Status: Crossed the Equator to enter the northern hemisphere
Weather: clear sky, 31º C, W 15 kts, 1m waves

Daily Position: N 1º 17' 59" E 103º 50' 43"
Status: In port Singapore, starboard side to
Weather: scattered clouds, humid, 34º C, wind and seas calm

Eight days at sea has given me an appetite for dry land, the storied and sandy islands of Singapore. The pilot comes aboard at zero six hundred. We enter the busy traffic separation lane of the Singapore Strait, and pass a hundred or more anchored vessels on our starboard side. One third of all global container traffic flows through here, the busiest trans-shipment point on earth.

My first visit is to the Botanic Gardens. Here $500 can buy a hybrid orchid crafted just for you, and then added to a garden with over 2,000 others named for VIPs including Princess Diana and Nelson Mandela. The 5.5 million citizens of this city-state revere greenery, and the first Sunday of every month is reserved for planting trees. Malaysian water sources are under constant political threat, so Singapore looks to purification and reuse, desalination, and "new water," requiring rain collection systems and green-planted rooftops for all new construction.

Chinatown is abustle with shoppers and hawkers of touristy gewgaws and sausages drying in the sun. It is already drenchingly hot by noon, with little wind to carry away the oppressive smell of rotting fish and offal. Ed grabs my hand and drags us in to the Tin Tin Shop on Pagoda Street. He has fond childhood memories of roaming the perilous pages of adventure with Hergé's comic hero and sidekick Snowy.

We step back into the street for delicate, subtle Chinese red bean and lotus pastries brushed with egg, then board the S-MRT to the Dhoby Ghaut station. We shop *Plaza Singapura* for honey, vegetables, and laundry detergent. I am on a quest for a yoga mat (too big to pack from home) and use my thumb to politely point out a nice one in lime green. The shop owner hands it down with a smile, and I force one in return. The heat has taken its toll, and yesterday's head cold now includes a headache.

Back aboard ship, we wiggle our way through a maze of anchored ships and out of port. Once just imagined, the Lion City has become a real memory.

Writing is an affair of yearning for great voyages and hauling on frayed ropes. ~ Israel Shenker

> *Remember that not getting what you want is sometimes a wonderful stroke of luck. ~ Dalai Lama XIV*

Port Kelang, Malaysia looks like the empty scrub of a Mississippi swampland, with a newish harbor terminal dropped on the bank, a barren pier jutting out, and not much else. The first Saturday of June is a national holiday: the King's birthday. Malaysia's Nine Sultans rotate the kingship every five years, so it may not be the actual king's birthday.

Ed and I catch a shuttle to the capital, Kuala Lumpur. Meaning *muddy estuary*, "KL" was carved out of the wilderness and planned from the start. It is now a jewel surrounded by jungle, wide and clean plazas setting off some of the tallest sparkling towers on the planet. Today is the first trip ashore with the collection of traveling objects, carried in a small black belt bag. At Petronas Towers, Ed photographs each object in turn. Locals grin as I pose with finger puppets and Lego bricks.

A national holiday brings two minor problems: public places are packed with locals enjoying a day off, and many regular attractions are closed. I wander through the Pusat Rekaan Kraft Centre in search of batik, a fabric dyed using a wax-resist technique. Most shops are shuttered for the holiday, sadly, but I visit artisans glazing pottery, hand-weaving scarves, and intricately carving wood.

All this time has been spent on foot, in the tropics, in the summertime. Properly and thoroughly wilted, I flag a cabbie, who battles holiday traffic to deliver me to the base of KL Tower. Waiting the line to purchase an elevator ride to the top would make me miss the outbound tide, so I settle for a slow (and air-conditioned) lunch at a quiet Indian restaurant and guzzle lots of bottled water.

I visit the World Honey Bee Museum, marvel at the huge hives on display, and spend my last Ringgits for "power honey" fortified with pollen and antioxidants. The afternoon ends with soft serve ice cream topped with peaches at City Centre's mall, *Signatures*. Under hazy skies, I vow to return on a future non-holiday.

Daily Position: N 3º 03' 47", E 101º 41' 10"
Status: In Port Kelang, Malaysia, starboard side-to
Weather: clear, 35º C, wind and seas calm

Daily Position: N 6º 25' 09" E 99º 49' 19"
Status: In port, Langkawi, Malaysia, starboard side-to
Weather: downpour, 35º C, NW 15 kts, 2 m waves

DAY 14

From the big city to Malaysia's western outpost we sail, taking northerly courses overnight up the Malacca Strait to the islands of Langkawi. It is said the legendary Garuda, half-human, half-eagle, once rested here, and named the place Helang- (eagle) -kawi (brown). Here, legends abound. One legend speaks of giants - brothers - who fought and spilled a huge pot of gravy over the town of Kuah (the Malay word for gravy). The most famous legend is of the beautiful Mahsuri who in 1819, wrongly accused of adultery, shed white blood at her execution. Innocence proven, she cast a curse with her final breath, to last for seven generations. The first child of the eighth was born in 1987, finally returning the island to prosperity.

LANGKAWI, MALAYSIA

Off-the-dock winds, stiff from the north-northwest, make mooring a protracted battle with lines and capstan. I am here at the start of the rainy season, and downpours arrive as blinding waterfalls with no warning. I am caught in the open while viewing the famous red sea eagles of the mangrove swamp, and find shelter under a plastic poncho. I still get drenched, but the temperature drops mercifully and I dry quickly. Ed commands the excursion from the bow of our small launch, speeding at 30 knots past basalt cliffs towering 100 meters above and tawny mangrove monkeys hunting crabs on the shore.

With four days at sea ahead, it is time for grocery shopping. An entire aisle of crisps sport flavors like prawn, crab, cuttlefish, and a mystery flavor "seafood." I am willing but Ed will not try any. A group of schoolgirls approach, shy and giggling, and ask for a photo with me. They are cute in their matching uniforms. Ed snaps pictures with their phones, a fun moment captured with "that silly American." I think they liked my hat.

JUNE 2

Our time ashore ends with a quick meal of dim sum, rice pudding and hot green tea. Ready for sea once again, we put the pilot ashore and set westerly courses across the top of the Malacca Straits toward the Indian Ocean.

Happiness is not a state to arrive at, but a manner of traveling.
-Anonymous (Backers Jenn and Jim Canfield)

Brewed from yesterday's wind and rain, we drive directly into line upon line of squalls. Squall lines are the birthplace of ocean waves. But the ship does not mind. She pushes deftly and with intention into and through each squall. We pass Banda Aceh on the northernmost point of Sumatra and proceed west out across the Indian Ocean.

Rain at sea, a trial by water. The decks pass from sprinkle to deluge and back again, wave upon wave of water from the sky. A cloudy noon position and into a darkening rain we plunge. Angry whitecaps pushed up by confused wavelets drive spray skyward in defiance of the downpour. The sea turns menacing and green.

Topside, droplets cover everything. Picking the wrong shoes is dangerous. Shoes with rubber soles are no longer optional. If a fitting is not watertight, the water comes in. Our observant crew is on the lookout for any surface without waterproofing, and adds it to the fair-weather work list. At sea, water is the supreme ruler. The wetness gets all over the decks, indiscriminately. Salt water always wins.

Underway rainstorms mean time spent moving around inside the skin of the ship. I avoid regular topside shortcuts in favor of staying dry, and encounter other passengers doing the same thing. The passageways are filled with "excuse me," "pardon me," "coming through," "oh, so sorry." Most take the voluntary incarceration in good spirits, though a few are quite put off by the weather. The clouds do not care. They just unleash the next waterfall of drops.

Clutches of passengers gather by portholes. Impromptu conversa-

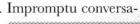

tions lead to evening plans, card games, and invitations to sing and dance. We are two weeks at sea. We are salty. We can do this circumnavigation "thing." What is a little bad weather? Just a signpost on the track line to adventure.

Engulfing the decks in darkness, the world returns to night, and the rain continues to fall.

Daily Position: N 6º 08' 02", E 092º 35' 20"
Status: Underway in the Malacca Straits & Indian Ocean
Weather: stormy & overcast, 27º C, SW 5 kts, 1.5 m waves

Daily Position: N 5° 34' 05" E 085° 55' 13"
Status: At Sea, Bay of Bengal, making 21 kts
Weather: high overcast, 28° C, W 35 kts, 6 m swells

DAY 16

BAY OF BENGAL

JUNE 4

Sri Lanka is in our sights. The Indian Ocean is the world's third largest, covering almost 20% of the earth's surface. It is bounded by Asia to the north, Africa to the west, Australia to the east and finally by the Southern Ocean. One quarter of the world's population lives in a country that borders the Bay of Bengal, there on our starboard side. On the water, we have smaller crowds.

The air is clear, and after yesterday's downpour the decks are awash with walkers, released from confinement and ready for exercise. One stroll around the promenade from stem to stern and back is just over 500 meters, so three laps make a mile. The pattern is counterclockwise but some brave souls go the other way, and are silently derided for their folly with squinted stares. The ocean is still choppy, and people do not so much jog as they stumble along in a general direction, trying desperately to avoid each other. Exercise like this would be comical if not necessary. Ed and I normally take four or five laps in the morning, before the crowds. We meet a couple training for a triathlon, who tell us of being scolded by the ship's purser for starting their runs before 7:00 a.m. Apparently the promenade deck is directly overhead his cabin.

Regular exercise is a smart part of routine, and my ship has a small area dedicated to fitness. Passengers can reserve a stationary bicycle, an elliptical machine, or a rowing machine. There are regular pick-up sessions for yoga and calisthenics. Push-ups and sit-ups can be done in the cabin, but just like lifting weights, the surging ship makes repetitions a challenge: one minute your body is extremely heavy, the next it is light as a feather. Weighing myself on a scale is more fun if I time the waves to get the best result.

To end the day, the ship hosts London Pub Night. Fish and chips, bangers and mash, and a couple pints of hearty stout serve to offset a conscientiously healthy day. Alone and in the dark, we round Sri Lanka and make a northwest turn to seek the west coast of India.

6

When you love what you have, you have everything you need.

As the days progress, I feel less urgency to clutch at every little experience. Anything I miss will come around again. I am settling comfortably into a new normal. Not vacationing here, but *living* here.

Our track takes us along a major traffic lane between the Persian Gulf and Suez Canal, and the Far East ports in our wake. We meet head-on or overtake a dozen vessels each hour. Most are huge container ships and tankers, but many are coastal freighters, tugs, and ferries.

The Captain does not miss the up-tick in traffic. He exercises the entire ship's company in Piracy Routine. All shipboard activities are limited. The bridge simulates an impending pirate attack, sounds alarms, and relays instructions over the public address system. We are directed to return to our cabin by internal routes and sit as far inboard as possible, away from exterior windows and doors. We prop open the interior cabin door to receive verbal instructions from the ship's crew. Finally we "secure from drill." This is a welcome announcement; it is annoying to be cooped up in a single spot at someone else's direction.

Customs officials from India's Bureau of Immigration have been aboard since our last port call. I fill out their paperwork. It is called "compulsory," which is a polite way of saying "if you want to go ashore, this had better be correct." Tomorrow we are scheduled for a face-to-face inspection with the officials, who may give us a landing card for Mumbai if everything is in order and they deem us worthy. My cold symptoms are starting to abate. Ed has the sniffles, but he should be able to pass inspection (and hopefully avoid quarantine).

Keeping ahead of laundry is an ongoing challenge. Involuntary confinement while avoiding simulated pirates does not help, but we each finish two loads of wash. Lonely Cape Comorin, the southern-most point of India, passes quietly down the starboard side as we slip into evening.

Daily Position: N 7º 11' 44", E 078º 12' 03"
Status: Underway, rounding Sri Lanka to Gulf of Mannar
Weather: Stormy then clear, 35º C, S 28 kts, 2 m swells

Daily Position: N 12º 56' 12" E 074º 17' 54"
Status: Approaches to Mumbai, various courses & speeds
Weather: showers & fog, 26º C, W 20 kts, 2 m waves

DAY 18

ARABIAN SEA

JUNE 6

E xcitement is building throughout the ship for tomorrow's stop at Mumbai, India. To leverage the high tides, we are scheduled to arrive at 11:00 a.m. after a three-hour transit, and sail again at 5:30 p.m. In this tight window, everything must run like clockwork. Messages flash back and forth to shore via satellite internet, to confirm details with the port husbanding agent for groceries and supplies, crew travel arrangements, diesel fuel, and other logistics.

The extra message traffic brings an already slow connection to a crawl. We pass beneath another storm front which brings "heavy seas on the beam," waves that hit our port side and cause large left-to-right rolls. Rolling just compounds the internet problem. Our stabilized antenna can't keep up with this extreme motion. I overhear other passengers "whinging" (griping) about the slowness, and while I sympathize, I secretly don't care. I love being informationally unplugged. It makes it easy to focus on the moment. The storms pass and gentle waves return.

U ntil now our country clearance and immigration encounters have gone smoothly. A three-month Indian tourist visa costs more than $200 per person with no guarantee of entry. After days of getting all worked up, the representatives ask only basic questions about my travel history, then present a yellow landing card. Some of our new Australian friends are still upset at the high price, for what will be a rushed six-hour port call. Ed and I will be heading overland for three days, and we start last-minute packing for the detour. Skirts, light clothes, sunscreen and bug repellent, closed-toe shoes, socks, umbrella, hand fan, hair brushes and hair bands all go into a single soft-sided red bag.

The military veterans hold a solemn memorial before the evening meal to mark the 69th anniversary of D-Day. Muted light from the city of Goa sheds a soft glow to our east, but a fiery setting sun and clouds of ochre and green - omens of sweltering heat for the weekend ahead - capture our attention.

When you talk, you are only repeating what you already know.
But if you listen, you may learn something new. ~ Dalai Lama

There is no happiness for the person who does not travel.
Indra is the friend of the traveler, therefore wander! ~ Brāhman

5

DAY 19

India assaults me at once with the stark, visceral contrast between stately beauty and complete filth. Wild dogs go about their business in the middle of downtown, sleep where they like, and scrounge for food in mounds of trash piled beneath gleaming monuments to famous Swamis and modern buildings rising in sheets of mirrored glass. People are everywhere, standing in silent groups and doing nothing. Mumbai's shores are littered with refuse, as are the sides of every street. There are too few trash bins, and those I spy overflow for lack of pickup.

At the Gateway of India near the storied Mumbai Hilton, savory hardwood smoke thickens the air. Tourists gawk, vendors hawk trinkets, and preteen children beg for coins. A dirty-faced boy reaches for my hand fan with a savvy air, as if expecting from long experience I will just pass it over. He makes no sound, just persistently gropes and clutches at my fan. When I do not relent, he makes a frustrated face and stalks off. A small girl carrying a baby ties a bracelet of jasmine flowers to my wrist and holds out her hand for payment. She looks confused and wants nothing to do with the $2 Australian coin I offer. Later I see her pass the coin to an older man, who scolds her, hands her more flower bracelets, and sends her back into the crowd.

We catch a bus to meet an outbound flight to New Delhi. Enroute to the field I am struck with regret: I can only see out one side! What wonders pass unseen on the *other* side? This is the nature of buses, and travel too. If passing through and never to return, pick the side upon which you sit with care. It makes a difference.

Daylight retreats behind the smog and dust of India's capital. We stop briefly at the India Gate, a prominent glowing marble arch, to remember 70,000 Indian soldiers who lost their lives with the British Army during World War I. Only here are there lights: elsewhere is darkness inside of blackness inside of night.

MUMBAI, INDIA

JUNE 7

Daily Position: N 18º 55' 18", E 072º 49' 52"
Status: In Port, Mumbai, India
Weather: high thin clouds, 32º C, W 5 kts, calm seas

Daily Position: N 20º 33' 54" E 067º 34' 42"
Status: Arabian Sea, heading NW for Gulf of Oman
Weather: overcast, 29º C, W 20 kts, 3 m waves

DAY 20

AGRA, INDIA

JUNE 8

The wake up call is early, too early. A hasty pack out and scramble for the bus, which picks its way through a dusty brown twilight to deposit me at the Delhi Railway Station. I board the Shatabdi Express towards Agra, in a car that is mercifully air-conditioned. The arrival platform is a swirl of humanity pressing to take my place, fine suits holding expensive cellphones mixing with the crutch-bound, breechclout-clad, less affluent. In a flash they are gone.

My goal is the Taj Mahal, as it opens, to avoid afternoon crowds. The windless heat is crushing and relentless. I am thankful for my wide straw hat and folding fan. Crafted by Emperor Shah Jahan to honor his beloved wife Arjumand Banu Begum, *The Taj* has been called "a teardrop of love, frozen in marble on the cheek of eternity." Framed by a scalloped arch, the spires, minarets and massive main dome glow in the mid-morning sunshine. At this distance the marble façade is textured white. I get closer and suddenly swirling organic patterns fixed in stone appear as if by magic. The surface is alive with gems from around the world, placed here, with love, almost 400 years ago. Twenty generations have tended and preserved this beauty, a love letter to the future.

I purchase a marble jewelry box inlaid using the same techniques and materials as decorate the Taj Mahal, and a sari (dress) embroidered in turquoise and violet. My next stop is the Red Fort, a sprawling complex augmented over centuries by each new conquering ruler. There is no repetition and no symmetry, a pleasing jumble of wide plazas and hidden secrets. One room is tiled floor to ceiling with broken mirrored glass, the "crystal room." The eastern parapet frames my last look at the world's most famous mausoleum.

Ed and I enjoy a relaxing meal of vegetable tandoori, as local Kathak performers dance to music played on harmonium and dholak drums. Swirling and green, a dervish dancer makes my eyelids feel heavy and, returning to my room, I find sleep with ease.

Anything worth doing is worth overdoing.
~ Mick Jagger

34

> *I will not let anyone walk through my mind with their dirty feet.*
> *~ Mahatma Gandhi*

Fully refreshed, I swing out of bed and realize why there is no carpet in the room: in a pre-summer blast furnace, bare feet on tile helps cool you down. Breakfast is fruit and vanilla pancakes and heavenly dark-pressed coffee. An express bus to the capital, and glimpses: a half-wet dog, a tuk-tuk burdened with chickens, bamboo scaffolding ten stories high, a rhesus macaque family escaping over rooftops with stolen bananas. And bricks - bricks everywhere. I should buy stock in Indian bricks.

The bus breaks down at the halfway point. A dozen men gather, open the hatch, gesture, pose, and ponder. A call goes out. A truck driver returns with two random handfuls of hardware. Our driver picks something, applies the fix, and we are back on the road. What odds: that particular trucker with that particular bolt at that particular stop at that particular moment? A million-dollar bolt. Karma.

Before lunch we stop at Jama Masjid, the largest and best-known mosque in India. A happy girl dances in the courtyard across a patch of corn spread for the pigeons. At the gate, we switch shoes for white slippers and Ed pays a 300 Rupee fee for his camera. I am wearing a hand-stamped yellow cotton dress, sunglasses, and a black veil over my hat. Mismatched western garb and gizmos on straps: we look ridiculous. Hometown visitors ask for pictures with me. I am clearly out of place and somehow this makes me famous. Famous enough.

Ed hails a red bicycle rickshaw and hands me up under the white canvas canopy. Our driver seems to find every pothole. And he seems to be fueled by tips. Ed puts the pedal down with a 100 Rupee note, and repeats the process every couple of blocks.

Near the entrance to Mahatma Gandhi's memorial flame, we buy bindis and take photos with a "tame" hooded cobra. The solemn shrine contrasts sharply with the bustle of the street, but the man whose memory is preserved here would approve of today's India, I think.

Daily Position: N 24º 15' 02", E 060º 04' 06"
Status: Arabian Sea, heading NW for Gulf of Oman
Weather: Partly cloudy, 32º C, S 10 kts, 1m waves

Sailing
Segment
Two

Daily Position: N 24º 57' 02" E 055º 20' 32"
Status: In Port, Dubai, U.A.E. port-side to pier 31/32
Weather: Hazy, 33º C, SW 9 kts, harbor calm

DAY 22

DUBAI, U.A.E

JUNE 10

Here I stand at 1:00 a.m., in the chaotic check-in queue. After an hour, I start 90 more minutes to clear customs, then board an Emirates flight to reconnect with the ship.

Dubai was once well known for pearls, until the Japanese cultured variety undercut prices. Since 1971 the seven states have focused on trade. Ten of the world's fifty tallest buildings are here, including the number one, Burj Khalifa, spiraling up 160 stories to challenge the sky. Unapologetic opulence, luxury, and excess abound: you can sprawl on a beach in the morning, then ski an *indoor* black diamond in the afternoon.

Pay attention to etiquette. Cover your knees. Do not show the bottoms of your feet. Never greet someone with your left hand. Always eat with the thumb and first two fingers of your right hand. No drugs, alcohol, or public displays of affection. Foul language will get you incarcerated. I am conscious of unconscious habits and am on my best behavior.

At the Al Bastakiya historic district I discover the wisdom of the original architects, who put tall buildings close together. Each building casts a cooling shadow over walkers on the ground, and the narrow winding streets help to strengthen feathery breezes. Ed is most impressed by a 19th century cooling tower powered by convection, then has to drag me away from the Dubai Museum's dense collection of artifacts and full-size dioramas depicting life for the city's early nomads.

We board a traditional dhow crossing Dubai Creek from the historic west bank to the more modern Deira neighborhood, and step ashore in the heart of the gold and spice souks. I am in a master chef's heaven of exotic spices in overflowing bins, of every variety, color, and scent.

A dust storm is darkening the sky to the west, so I gather my purchases and race for the ship. The pilot is aboard to set northeasterly courses up the gulf coast for the Straits of Hormuz. Driven to sea, the bow meets a sharp horizon, dust engulfs the city, and in our wake, gray spires are swallowed by the sand.

5

Our battered suitcases were piled again; we had longer ways to go. But no matter. The road is life. ~ Jack Kerouac

> Many times the wrong train took me to the right place.
> ~ Paulo Coelho Aleph

5♦

Overnight we exited the Persian Gulf to enter the Gulf of Oman. Being at sea does not temper the heat. Topside metal decks bake and radiate sweltering waves like an oiled griddle. The stagnant air is steamy and sauna-thick with moisture.

We have set a southeasterly course throughout the morning across the Gulf of Oman, threading our way between inbound tankers and an occasional container ship. Four days of adventure have taken their toll: Ed has a blazing headache and spends most of the day in agony. Right on cue at 7:00 a.m., the deck crew begins a grinding project on our cabin's exterior bulkhead. I bring Ed strong coffee and bubble packs of Indian ibuprofen.

We cross the Tropic of Cancer in the afternoon and alter course to the southwest to round Ras al Hadd on the far eastern coast of Oman. The event passes unseen by many of the "new hands" we picked up yesterday. They are still trying to settle in, find everything, and get their sea legs. It is actually kind of funny to watch. I think back just three short weeks to my first days aboard and see how *I* must have looked. Walking the passageways I am again mistaken for a member of the crew, several times. What does it take to be considered an "old hand"? With a confident air I could send one of these new souls off to fetch a piece of shoreline or a bucket of prop wash.

This segment will be the longest and most activity-filled leg of the trip, through the Holy Land, eastern and western Mediterranean, and Western Europe. Our next port call at Safaga, Egypt is the first of 18 stops. My gear is shaken down, broken in, and ready, but first I must pass five warm days at sea, locked to the trackline, through (reportedly) pirate-infested waters. I plan to spend the time getting caught up on my journal and organizing photos.

Our return from India confers us celebrity status, so we regale our dinner companions with tales of monkeys, temples, and bricks.

Daily Position: N 23º 06' 06", E 059º 29' 02"
Status: On a southeast course to cross the Tropic of Cancer
Weather: Hazy & hot, 32º C, NE 9 kts, 3 m waves

Daily Position: N 16º 59' 36" E 055º 59' 42"
Status: Southwest course to parallel the coast of Oman
Weather: overcast, 28º C, W 24 kts, 4 m waves

DAY 24

The Gulf of Oman greets our passage with a stiff westerly blow and regular waves on the starboard beam. The ship is really moving. I am not the only one getting around by means of the hand-over-hand technique. The crew rigs extra lifelines to help with safely while topside, rough brown manila and smooth yellow nylon. Briney spray is stripped from wave tops to splatter warm droplets on my face. My lips taste salt and my skin tightens against the onslaught. Spray coats the teak, making my fore-and-aft mid-morning walk a flip-flop of traction. The shaded starboard deck is damp and therefore feels sticky underfoot, an easy grip for rubber soles.

The deck pitches more violently as I approach the bow. Instinctively, my left hand reaches out to grasp the metal handrail and comes back coated in gritty crystals. Spritz upon spritz of brine evaporates and leaves a layered, crusty patina over every open surface. I start aft down the port side. There is less spray here on the eastern and leeward (downwind) side. The sunlit deck is warm and dry and the salt crystals become like miniature ball bearings, a thin and caustic layer of slippery powder.

ARABIAN SEA

As we move in and out of shadow throughout the day, metal fixtures and bulkheads expand and contract, opening micro-cracks in the thick white paint. Small weld seams gather salt, which corrodes the bare steel beneath. Oxidized brown slurry oozes out, leaving telltale running rust. Staying ahead of corrosion is a daily battle for the deck crew.

Fearing pirates, the ship stations crewmembers topside to watch for any inbound threat from small, fast boats with evil intent. Mounted on each of the four quarters, long-range acoustic devices, "sonic canons," are poised to dissuade boarders with an uncomfortable low frequency blast. We hug the northern shore of the Gulf of Aden to avoid the hotbed of Somali pirates, staying close to Oman and Yemen. Nighttime steaming, lookouts with binoculars, and big black speakers will be our salvation.

JUNE 12

The fear of death follows from the fear of life. A man who lives fully is prepared to die at any time. ~ Mark Twain

> *Mistakes are proof that you are trying.*

Our southwesterly course brings us ever closer to Bab el-Mandeb, the narrow entrance of the Red Sea. Two dozen days ago we left Australia behind. Each day I feel more at home aboard our floating oasis. Even the regular sparring for laundry machines feels like routine. Ed has an amusing exchange with the ship's engineer, who insists there are no parts on board to fix a faulty dryer outflow hose. Ed offers to join him in the ship's machine shop and manufacture a replacement himself. Within two short hours a heavy-duty replacement hose is "discovered" and installed, putting our weekly laundry operations back on track.

Part of settling in to a new place is discovery of the hidden, off-the-beaten-track spots, known only to locals. Ed has a quiet nook where he spends most mornings with coffee and journal, cataloging our trip; I enjoy reading in a back corner of the ship's central commons. Every space has several uses throughout the day, so what starts as a quiet and private retreat could suddenly be transformed into a lecture hall, or a loud and boisterous emergency drill for passengers and crew. Outside our cabin, nowhere is ever reliably private. This is very likely by design, to keep people moving, on their toes, and ready for anything.

As full circumnavigation travelers, we have earned a low-level "Captain's Circle" status. One of the eventual benefits will be free laundry, but that is reserved for passengers who have made several more trips with this company. Still, even low-level status comes with a few perks. We meet the captain and enjoy a glass of champagne at a small reception. With three decades at sea, he seems not at all concerned by the pirates, fully confident in his ship and the preparations of his crew.

Dinner is ceviche salad, a well-seasoned plate of shrimp and rice, and a moist chocolate cake. Enchanting Arabian stars sparkle as we join a lively deck party to share drinks, tall tales, and the start of another night at sea.

Daily Position: N 13º 09' 30", E 048º 46' 24"
Status: International transit corridor to avoid pirate activity
Weather: Sunny with haze, 32º C, SW 14 kts, 1 m waves

Daily Position: N 14º 53′ 31″ E 041º 54′ 48″
Status: Underway with Eritrea to port, Yemen to starboard
Weather: Hazy & Hot, 32º C, W 19 kts, sea calm

DAY 26

Into the early morning fog we sail, to transit Bab el-Mendeb - the narrow entrance into the Red Sea separating Djibouti and Eritrea on our port side and Yemen on our starboard side. The Red Sea is a major shipping corridor. I see mid-sized cargo ships hauling a kaleidoscope of neatly stacked containers, and giant tankers moving petrol from the Arabian sands to Europe. As expected, this area of the world is well patrolled by concerned naval forces. One man-of-war stands out for carrying a Dauphin helicopter like Ed once flew for the U. S. Coast Guard. The bridge thinks it is a Saudi destroyer.

Managing a fleet of electronic gadgets is an expected part of travel. Our photographs come from seven cameras: two in our mobile phones; two low quality clip-on cameras; a dedicated SLR-style; a point-and-shoot; and as backup of last resort, a high-definition video camera. Ed moves photos to his 15" laptop for storage, cataloging, and editing. I maintain ship-to-shore correspondence with my 13" laptop.

RED SEA

The best camera is always the one you have with you, but if the battery is empty then the shot will be lost. Keeping the batteries for all these devices full and service-ready is an ongoing dance with the plug. We have along a four-outlet power splitter, two international plug adapters, and special adapters for our laptops. The Australian-based ship has most outlets configured for 240 volt Australian, and the occasional 120 volt U. S.-style. Ed checked each piece of gear back in the States for compatibility with "world power," but there was no way to know if something would work until actually plugging it in. We are fortunate to have had reliable power and (so far) no hiccups.

JUNE 14

The ship's senior officers say this area of the world is notorious for today's real problem: a glacially slow internet connection. The satellites sit over India and the central Mediterranean and we are precisely in the middle, on the fringe of both. Nothing we can do to shift them, so our outbound data is at their mercy.

May you always have fair winds & following seas,
as you did on this trip! (Backers Joe & LaRae Malinauskas)

As our Kenyan friends say, "Safe safari!" in all your travels.
(Backers The Wilson Family - All 10 of us)

7

Out of touch with the world, we take time to overhaul our gear. Tomorrow marks the start of scheduled visits to 18 ports in only 28 days, a blistering pace. We are determined to capture this once-in-a-lifetime experience from start to finish, and photography is a big part of that. With so many opportunities for pictures, it will be difficult to avoid viewing each port through the camera lens.

Ed has adopted an almost paranoid mania about preserving our captured memories. He brought along a storage device that has four hard drives linked together for capacity. The hard drives also mirror each other, preserving all files if any one drive fails. Our two computers carry original copies and are backed up daily to the storage drive and a second hard drive. The collection is already 3,500 photos strong, and we are barely a quarter-way around the planet.

Edward's tenacity means I can focus on this experience. I never thought I would be able to do much traveling. My first inspiration for travel came from my mother's sister, Aunt Dotty. She traveled the world, often missing my birthday celebrations. When she returned, we would project stacks of picture slides on a big screen and listen to amazing stories of her trips. She brought belated birthday gifts from around the world. Aunt Dotty was killed by a drunk driver when I was ten years old. Still, I will never forget her enthusiasm for travel. My parents also traveled, to support my father as he swam in long distance marathons, sometimes in a protective cage through shark-infested waters. They made trips to England when Dad was part of relay teams swimming the English Channel.

My battle with brain cancer has refocused so many priorities. I hope my decision to sail the world will inspire others - you - to prioritize travel in this life. Telling my tale is now my real purpose, my obsession. Onward I sail, because the world is just the start.

Daily Position: N 21º 54' 12", E 037º 38' 30"
Status: Underway, following coast of Saudi Arabia to stbd
Weather: Sunny, scattered, 30º C, NW 24 kts, choppy seas

Daily Position: N 26º 44' 02" E 033º 56' 32"
Status: In Port, Safaga, Egypt, port-side to
Weather: clear, 32º C, N 25 kts, 1 m chop

DAY 28

LUXOR, EGYPT

JUNE 16

Africa greets us with a dark blue and cloudless sky. Daily life in the port is a constant battle with traffic, construction, and dust. I head west through the Safaga Mountains, in search of the Nile River, a thin green strip dividing the tawny desert. Trade in wheat brought gold and jewels that fueled glittering dynasties for 3,000 years. In the sand, roots seeking water grow deep: 99 of every 100 Egyptians still live within a mile of these shores.

I wave to a family out on their morning commute, riding in the bed of a salvaged pickup truck being pulled by a donkey. Life along Luxor's East Bank thrives by this marriage of new and old technology: electric lights in homes built with mud daub bricks, 55-gallon barrel lids on traditional amphora-shaped clay ovens, posters for Coca-Cola over storefronts built from reclaimed planks. The markets offer date palms, bananas, sugar cane, and grapes in overflowing bins. Patient veil-clad mothers in ochre and green watch children laugh and play in the Nile.

Crossing to the West Bank, I escape the sun under one of the mythical Colossi of Memnon, 20 meters tall. My next stop is the Valley of the Kings. There is no shade, so Ed opens an umbrella as we trudge south up a scree slope of chipped limestone, a meandering *wadi*. I am allowed to visit three tombs but must leave my camera behind. The spectacular sarcophagus of Pharaoh Seti II lies before me in a tomb dug deep from the living rock of a near-vertical cliff. Osiris, adorned in blue, red, and brilliant gold, still guards these chilly halls with a piercing gaze.

My last stop is the Temple of Luxor, built by Amenhotep in the 16th century BC and expanded by other pharaohs, including Ramses II. A striking Avenue of Sphinxes leads to the temple gate, marked by a red granite obelisk which, when compared to its weathered twin in Paris, boasts carvings still distinct after 3,000 years. Western sunlight fades, and the temple's textured pillars continue their rigid vigil, guarding untold secrets of antiquity.

Not to know is bad. Not to wish to know is worse.
~ African Proverb

> *I have not told half of what I saw.*
> *~ Marco Polo*

Black Bedouin tents dot the scrubby wheat-covered tableland, 5,600 feet above sea level on Jordan's Mountain Heights plateau. Bedouin nomads, the people here, live much as their ancestors did in the time of the spice trade - a simple life of herding and harvesting grains by hand. They shelter under dark tents made of fabric woven from the wiry goat wool of the native Dhaiwi, and this is on purpose. The dark hairs warm in the sun, expand and stretch, and open the tent to airy breezes. Wild grasses are plentiful, an impressive amount of green for a country that gets only 100 centimeters of rain each year.

East of Petra I leave the King's Highway and approach The Siq on foot. The path is well worn by travelers and horses shod in steel. Dusty. Traders vie for spots, enticing visitors to the Lost City with motley, scarves, and trinkets. Every object is unique, and all are of local craft. **R**elentless midday sun beats down as my sweaty steps take me past the Djinn blocks, six meters on a side and each carved from a solid sandstone boulder. They may have served as meteorological observation posts, or tombs and monuments to the dead.

A cooler wind carries the smell of horse and camel dung to this end of the high-walled siq. I use part of my black head scarf to block the scent. The confining red passage narrows and blocks the sun, but reflects painful echoes from passing horse carts. In contrast, a pair of camels pass silently by, marked only by their fetid stench. I gag, pull my scarf tighter across my face, and am glad the beasts are quickly gone.

Like a child peeking from its mother's skirts, the fabled Treasury façade becomes visible around a bend in the canyon. I must soon retrace my steps, but here with mouth agape, I stand transfixed before a true wonder of the world. To describe the 2,000 year old Nabatean craftwork would be impossible. Their legacy is locked in time, a vision frozen in the stone.

Daily Position: N 29º 31' 00", E 035º 00' 00"
Status: In Port, Aqaba, Jordan, starboard-side to
Weather: Clear, 30º C, NE 19 kts, calm seas

Daily Position: N 27º 23' 42" E 034º 24' 36"
Status: Straits of Tiran to Red Sea, holding for Suez transit
Weather: clear, 28º C, NW 15 kts, 2 m waves

DAY 30

Heading through the Strait of Tiran this morning, we re-enter the Red Sea, then alter course to the north-northwest and enter the Gulf of Suez before midday.

The bridge team keeps us safe from collision with cargo vessels in the busy lanes converging at this global choke point. They keep a regular rotation of "watches" so each officer can complete other duties, and get some sleep. At 8:00 p.m. the 2000 to 0000 or *first watch* sees the easing-down time for the crew, when daily work is done and equipment is set for safe steaming or sailing overnight. The 0000 to 0400 or *middle watch* is the slowest. Emergency drills and work tasks are not scheduled during this time, as those not on watch are asleep. The 0400 to 0800 is the morning or *navigator's watch*. Ed likes this watch the best. The navigator is up to check progress along the trackline overnight, to take the morning sun line, calculate a position, and set courses for the upcoming day. Breakfast starts below decks and the ship comes alive during the 4-to-8. The 0800-1200 *forenoon watch* marks the start of the workday, with drills, exercises, and scheduled maintenance. Noon bells start the *afternoon watch* until 1600, a continuation of the regular work day. The *first dog watch* from 1600 to 1800 is a break from the regular four hour schedule, so those on watch can get evening chow, replaced from 1800 to 2000 by the *second dog watch*. And the cycle repeats, day upon day. A ship at sea is truly alive, and these regular watches are her pulse.

RED SEA

Hemmed in by Egypt's South Sinai governorate to starboard and the Suez governorate to port, we slow our speed to keep from arriving early at the Suez Canal. Topside is strangely quiet as the ship lingers

offshore for clearance. I spend a lovely evening relaxing on deck. To the west, Mercury and Venus chase each other into a horizon glowing ingot-hot with reflected dust. "Now" seems delightfully easy, as the bridge officers continue their eternal vigil above. Unrushed, a warm breeze gently tugs my hair.

JUNE 18

Procrastination means never having to say you're sorry until tomorrow.

46

> *The greatest pleasure in life is doing what people say you cannot do.*
> *~ Walter Bagehot*

ings as far back as Senusret II and Ramesses II had dreamed of a water route between the Red Sea and the Mediterranean. There may have been an ancient canal from a branch of the Nile eastward to the Red Sea, but a channel through Suez remained only an idea. The French military expedition to Egypt in 1798 again raised the possibility: a shortened route to India would open a vast empire in the east.

Napoleon's occupation of Egypt was short, and nothing was done. The French public had become enchanted with the idea, however. Despite predictable British opposition, engineer Ferdinand de Lesseps gained permission from Said Pasha, the Khedive (viceroy) of Egypt, to found the International Suez Canal Company, and dig from the Mediterranean coast to the town of Suez on the Red Sea. He would incorporate several depressions in the desert, now called the Bitter Lakes. The Isthmus of Suez is less than 100 miles of open desert, still a formidable task for workers with shovels. The first ship to pass through was *L'Aigle* in November 1869, and a long procession of 68 ships from many nations followed, with much fanfare. The Canal rapidly became a commercial triumph, and the Canal Company grew wealthy.

A surprise: the Suez Canal has no locks. It is just a straight cut through from sea to sea. The entire length of the canal is flanked by military outposts, each an oasis for watchers along the banks. This duty seems an uncomfortable, no-joke affair: locked in a tower open to the desert, the only entertainment a parade of floating steel. Near the northern terminus I spot wreckage of tanks destroyed during the October war of 1973, a grim reminder of past tensions that may still resurface. Locals take to the canal in rowboats with bait and pole, much like weekend fishermen do back home. The canal is their backyard, and I am just another interloper passing through. Rocking in our wake as we pass, they wave and cast again.

> **Daily Position:** N 30º 37' 36", E 032º 19' 36"
> **Status:** Northbound, day transit of Suez Canal
> **Weather:** Clear sky, 30º C, N 15 kts, canal water calm

Daily Position: N 31º 48' 02" E 034º 39' 32"
Status: In port, Ashdod, Israel, port-side to
Weather: clear & hazy, 26 C, WSW 9 kts, calm

DAY 32

Jerusalem is spread out below me in a sea of layered memories, the Holy Land. The Dome of the Rock gleams in a piercing beam of morning sunlight. Cross-topped spires shed long shadows across densely packed cubes, each with a water tank and satellite dish. Flowers of red and purple waft their sweet fragrance aloft, coating the dewy air, a western-slope dampness that does not last.

Over the ridge goes my bus, a winding journey down, down, down into the Jordan Valley, bound for the Dead Sea. An aquamarine sign proudly proclaims Sea Level in white letters, English and Hebrew. And I continue down, ears popping, to a West Bank security checkpoint. A woman sporting chest-length braided hair and a tightly slung M-16 rifle gives the green light to enter Qumran National Park. At 430 meters (1,400 feet) below sea level, breathing is easy, the air dense and salty.

The best way to visit Masada is by funicular from the valley and back to sea level at the top. Here at King Herod's well-stocked fortress, a small group of Sicarii rebels withstood a two-year siege before committing mass suicide in the year 73. I tour a spectacular bathhouse, colorful Roman mosaics covering the walls. Water was heated below, piped in, and steam would rise through vertical tubes to escape small holes throughout the room. Back in the sun, I peer into the valley at the outline of eight Roman camps from the siege, surrounded by chortling tiny ravens who flash iridescent black and desert tan feathers.

Lunch is a vinegared affair of hummus and saged wheat bread: crisp, thin outer crust, inside soft and moist. I trade street clothes for a swimsuit, and race painfully barefoot across crusty, burning salt crystals to the inland sea. My skin fights the brine, and feels covered in an oil that will not wash off. It is so hard to keep my feet down! Stray drops taste bitter on my tongue, and I guard my eyes. After an hour I wash off and, giggling at the experience, sip espresso. Nothing is the same after you've swum in the Dead Sea.

MASADA & THE DEAD SEA   JUNE 20

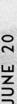

Certainly, travel is more than the seeing of sights; it is a change that goes on, deep and permanent, in the ideas of living. ~ Mary Ritter Beard

Ranging wide, mythical mariners from antiquity sailed the eastern Mediterranean, seeking riches and glory. Monsters unknown, epic storms, battles with gods and demigods, tales of loves won and lost, all made their mark among the scattered islands in the Sea of Crete.

To be human is to yearn for the sea. It is part of our shared global mythos. It is in our blood. Upon these waters our ancestors encountered new peoples, new ideas, learned the ways of sail and current, spread culture and civilization, and waged war. Sailors in ships great and boats tiny set out into the unknown, leaving those they loved behind, grasping at promises only Poseidon could fulfill. Lost in the swirling whirlpools along the rocky, earthquake-torn shores of these thousand islands, the details can never be known. I pass in silence and shiver at the echoes of a million stories strung across millennia.

Noon reports. The Captain reminds us it is the longest day of the year. Eight time zones are in our wake, with sixteen more to go. A relaxing day at sea is just what I need to recover from three sweltering port calls, and prepare for three more. To the laundry, with the regular drama of chasing machines and massaging the coin-operated levers. Ed uploads photographs for the benefit of family and friends, and makes a satellite call to check on his aging grandmother. The news is not good, and he is frustrated to be "stuck" here and not with the family in what may be her last days. They are all very close.

To take our minds off news from home, we attend lectures about the upcoming ports of Athens, Mytilene, and Istanbul. Parts of the Turkish city are in flames as protesters battle police who cleared Gezi Park with water cannons and tear gas on June 15th. Our berth will be far from the protests, and we will hold to our itinerary, but watch the news. Travelers upon an ancient sea, connected nomads with modern concerns - an enchanting mix indeed.

Daily Position: N 35º 05' 04", E 028º 49' 51"
Status: Underway westbound in the eastern Mediterranean
Weather: Clear sky, 26º C, WNW 8 kts, 1 m waves

Daily Position: N 37º 58' 32" E 023º 43' 26"
Status: In Port, Piraeus, Greece, starboard-side to
Weather: Clear sky, 28º C, NE 15 kts, calm water

DAY 34

ATHENS, GREECE

JUNE 22

Piraeus harbor welcomes us to Greece on an early morning tide. This is the first port with Euros as currency. The cash machine is my first stop, a better exchange rate than the ship's purser, guaranteed.

The wind atop the Acropolis is from the north and relentless, stirring up sand and grit. Millions of dusty footsteps have ground any piece of exposed marble to a fine polish. Footing is slippery. Ed poses our globetrotting objects on the east side of the Parthenon. A tabby cat greets me, her fur the color of the surrounding marble. She gratefully drinks water from my hand.

We leave the summit and happen upon the octagonal Horologion of Kyrrhestos, the Tower of the Winds. I discover an archaeological museum with (easily) 500 pieces of pottery on display. I photograph everything. The modern camping industry could take hints from this Hellenic period cookware. A grandfatherly docent shows me a picture of himself as a toddler, modeling one unlikely find: a 2,000 year-old bathroom training chair. The ancient design has not changed.

Lost on the outskirts of the Plaka and getting hungry, Ed spots a sign for Taverna Sissifos. Under a natural arbor of ripening grapes, I order eggplant lasagna, stuffed grape leaves drenched in creamy melted goat cheese, pumpkin balls prepared like falafel, and Greek salad, all chased with Coca-Cola from a real glass bottle. Then dessert: heavenly baklava laced with clove, the bottom pastry layer so steeped in honey it has the consistency of waxed paper that melts just in time to let the texture of finely chopped walnuts tickle my tongue. And my tongue begs for bite after bite until every morsel is devoured.

Descending to the Plaka shops, I buy comfortable, handmade leather sandals to replace a worn out set. Masks, musical instruments, dresses, jewelry: anything can be found here. I finish the day with a latte and pastry before catching a shuttle to the ship. Ornate marble columns lie toppled alongside the street.

A journey is a person in itself; no two are alike. We find after years of struggle that we do not take a trip; a trip takes us. ~ John Steinbeck

50

> *If you always do what interests you, at least one person is pleased.*
> ~ *Katharine Hepburn*

Mytilene is the capital of the Greek island of Lesbos. The city's shallow harbor means the ship must anchor out. I catch a shorebound tender boat and walk first by the Liberty Statue, silent and striking in bronze atop a gleaming white marble pedestal, sadly marked with graffiti. I follow a closed, paved road north out of town to a small lighthouse on the island's eastern point, built to resemble a fishing boat.

A pack of stray, purebred dogs follows me around the next bend to Mytilene Castle, an abandoned fortress. The castle is being repaired in stages. On Sunday, the site has no activity. There are no barriers, signs, or security guards to keep me out. I scramble around the entire restoration area, almost certainly in violation of occupational health and safety regulations, and discover a gigantic kiln for firing clay pots and large ceramics. It is obvious the builders will use it once the rework is complete. At the base of the fort, five-petaled purple wildflowers and tiny red poppies cover the hillside.

Ed inspects a sailboat on display, impressed by stabilizing outriggers built into the hull. The design is perfect for dragging ashore on shallow secluded island beaches. I peek through the windows of a recently restored Greek Orthodox Church; gold leaf glitters back.

I settle on a cafe and sit by the water. The staff ignores me for five minutes, which gives time to catch my breath, watch the small fish battling the shoreside swells, and enjoy the onshore breeze. They bring ouzo, a local anise-flavored alcohol, and I order fava bean dip topped with purple onions. The bread is fresh baked and exactly the way I like it: crust thin with a sprinkle of flour and a lingering hint of yeast in pockets of non-uniform texture. Greek coffee arrives sweetened only "medium." The cuppa is a veritable dessert by itself. For his meal, Ed savors a plate of grilled sardines, very likely cousins to those darting in the surf, and declares this to be a perfect day.

Daily Position: N 39º 05' 58", E 026º 39' 13"
Status: Riding starboard anchor, Island of Lesvos, Greece
Weather: Sky clear, 28º C, NNW 7 kts, 1 m waves

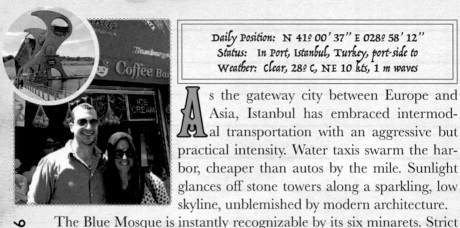

Daily Position: N 41º 00' 37" E 028º 58' 12"
Status: In Port, Istanbul, Turkey, port-side to
Weather: clear, 28º C, NE 10 kts, 1 m waves

DAY 36

ISTANBUL, TURKEY

JUNE 24

As the gateway city between Europe and Asia, Istanbul has embraced intermodal transportation with an aggressive but practical intensity. Water taxis swarm the harbor, cheaper than autos by the mile. Sunlight glances off stone towers along a sparkling, low skyline, unblemished by modern architecture.

The Blue Mosque is instantly recognizable by its six minarets. Strict proctors enforce the dress code. I must remove my shoes and cover my head and shoulders. Men must cover their legs and remove their hats. Called "blue" because of the ornate blue tile, mosaics cover every inch of the cavernous interior. Images of people or animals are reserved for the creator. Mere human hands are limited to geometric and floral patterns, or the written word. Hundreds of bare feet tread this carpet every day. The not-quite-overpowering smell screams, "Time for a cleaning!"

Closer to the old city, I visit a craft center specializing in knotted rugs of cotton, wool, and silk. A young woman demonstrates knotting tight patterns with colored shimmering threads. Size alone does not set the price. It is time, influenced by thread count and complexity. Large Turkish rugs can take over a year of work by two skilled craftspeople. The shop patron offers us licorice-flavored raki. "First shot, you feel like a sultana. The second reveals your hidden talents. Third and you speak fluent Turkish. Fourth and you do not stand or walk straight." And the fifth, I ask? "Then you see the flying carpets." Just one, please.

In the Grand Bazaar, you can find anything with enough searching, if you can tolerate the pungent and intermingled spicy scents. At the Joker Büfé near Gate #1, I order Turkish coffee from Daniel, the 25-year-old proprietor. He grew up in Seattle and prefers Starbucks, but has embraced Turkey's vibrant startup culture with plans for a chain of cafés. He offers a variety plate of Turkish Delight rolled in powdered sugar; lemon, orange, and mint. A dusty piece shimmers on my green plastic fork as I nibble.

5

The world always seems brighter when you've just made something that wasn't there before. ~ Neil Gaiman

> Find out who you are and do it on purpose.
> ~ Dolly Parton

Overnight we transit the narrow Dardanelli Strait and turn north to drop anchor at 6:00 a.m. in Anzac Cove. A regal, brown-speckled grasshopper buzzes aboard from the greening shores of Gallipoli. Many passengers have family ties to soldiers who fought or were lost in battle here, during an abominable eight-month campaign that began April 25, 1915 with a dawn attack into a blinding sunrise. Almost 27,000 Australian and New Zealand Army Corps (ANZAC), British, and French Allied troops set up camp on the shore. Ordered to conquer the Ottoman forts that had wrested control over the Dardanelles, the well-matched forces met in battle, and thousands were lost on both sides.

At 8:00 a.m., the bugle calls and we hold a moving daybreak service, drifting in the cove. The Captain presides over official readings, a brief history, and rings a ceremonial bell in remembrance of the fallen. Laying a wreath upon the waters is a customary tradition, but the government of Turkey has declined our request and the wreath stays aboard. Ed has been singing with the passenger choir and participates in that capacity, a haunting rendition of a song called The Prayer. One talented passenger sings a solo performance of Waltzing Matilda, building verse upon verse until every eye is wet with tears. This story is not part of history texts in the States, but today I am transformed by the service, and feel the pain of loss that for many is still all too real.

Lunch is a British pub buffet, with obligatory fish and chips, plus curried chicken, and bangers and mash. I attend port briefings for upcoming stops in Naples and Rome, then grab a quick siesta.

Our regular evening tablemates discuss the various annoying foibles of other passengers. We agree none of *us* are annoying in the slightest, and vow a nightly toast to ourselves will henceforth be in order. Clinking glasses set this new tradition in the fading light, as the Spartan peninsula passes away to starboard.

Daily Position: N 37º 54' 58", E 024º 34' 45"
Status: Position keeping, Anzac Cove
Weather: light scattered, 30º C, NE 13 kts, 1 m waves

DAY 38

Crossing the Ionian Sea leads us around the southernmost point of Italy. The bridge team is kept busy by tiny boats and narrow channels. Twice, they embark pilots to navigate shallow, tight passes between rocky islands.

The ship's deck and engineering teams do not slouch, either. Days at sea are normally a bit more laid back, but we are over a month away from homeport, and the work list is starting to pile up. In the Mediterranean Sea the waves are predictably calm, there is less salt spray, and any over-the-side maintenance can be done safely. Small equipment breakages or "casualties" are addressed. The deck force preps and paints spots of running rust.

An entire team descends upon the weather deck outboard rails with scraper, sanding blocks, and varnish to get a jump on corrosion. The rails are dark wooden - layered teak - and would probably do just fine without all the attention. But a chipping rail with dull varnish is just not acceptable for our erstwhile deckies. In a few short hours the scraping and sanding are done and wet paint signs are up along the entire port side rail. On Tuesday they will repeat the process on the starboard side.

IONIAN SEA

Yesterday's vow to make a regular toast has special meaning tonight, as tablemates Larraine and Bert are celebrating an anniversary. They are an inspiration: this is their third circumnavigation trip. Larraine declares, "Adventure before dementia!" We drink to this, and then the galley serves panna cotta with rum raisins and chocolate sauce. We lampoon the latest annoying passenger type, a new pariah: the electronic tablet photographer. Any old mobile device with a camera is not always the best choice, especially when your phototaking fully obscures the view of those behind you.

JUNE 26

We sail deftly up the west coast of Italy. The volcano on Stromboli Island makes a show, steam and smoke blown off the caldera by strong westerly winds. Eyes turned warily to port, I follow the glow of lava flowing down into the sea, then find my rack and turn in early.

3

The impossible often has a kind of integrity, which the merely improbable lacks. ~ Douglas Adams

54

When life hands you lemons, make limoncello.
~ Ed Beale

Ashore in Naples, today's multi-faceted trip starts in Sorrento for shopping, then lunch at a lemon, cheese, and olive farm, and finishes in Pompeii, prowling the excavated ancient city, destroyed in AD 79 by the famous Mount Vesuvius.

The route south to Sorrento snakes along the steep, west-facing cliffs. Eyes on the road and do not look down! In town I pick up new Italian words and restock my supply of fresh, local fruit. The bustle has a "resort-y" and relaxed feel; Europeans on holiday and decidedly Mediterranean. In the lemon groves at a hillside farm, I marvel at one-meter-diameter stone wheels. They have been crushing olives into oil for over 100 years, originally turned by a donkey and now by electric motor. The farm serves four types of cheese, three cured meats, two hearty breads, spaghettata olive oil, white wine, and limoncello shots: anise, chocolate, and cream. Everything on my plate was grown or pressed within 100 meters of the table. A fuzzy orange-eyed kitten in a copper rain spout cries for her share.

Pompeii is every bit as haunting as I had expected, a place dripping with dark memories, veiled by fate. Archaeologists have exposed two-thirds of the city from under a dozen meters of soil and ash. Gilded medallions in stucco relief decorate the domed ceiling of a first-century resort hotel. Elevated crosswalks in Pompeii kept pedestrian feet above the horse manure and refuse mingling in the streets. Gaps between step stones allowed cart wheels to pass. A detailed plaster imprint of an unfortunate inhabitant lies in a glass casket, his head cradled by his right forearm and composed for sleep. Curators are quick to remind me these are *not* human remains. Either way, he never knew tomorrow.

A chill comes over me. I turn and settle my gaze on the summit of Vesuvius, lurking up the street behind an ancient arch. Traveling back to the ship brings me unexpected relief: here aboard, I am safe from the next eruption.

Daily Position: N 40º 50' 36", E 014º 15' 46"
Status: In Port, Naples, Italy to visit Sorrento and Pompeii
Weather: fair cumulus clouds, 29º C, S 12 kts, 1 m waves

Daily Position: N 41º 40' 02" E 012º 42' 02"
Status: In port Civitavecchia, Italy to visit Rome
Weather: hazy but clear, 22º C, NW 10 kts, 1 m waves

DAY 40

ROME, ITALY

JUNE 28

Entering the harbor of Civitavecchia, the first thing I see is a three story building marked *Guardia Costiera* with a jaunty diagonal stripe, the Italian Coast Guard. Ed and I board a chartered train for Rome and a day of seeing the sights on foot. Rome is at the same latitude as our home, but the day is *hot*, as if we have traveled into more southern climes. The cooler Mediterranean breezes do not reach very far inland. Our train arrives in western Rome and within walking distance of St. Peter's Basilica. It is Friday and therefore not much going on in the square. The new Pope is still settling in.

Around the first corner is my kind of bookstore and the real reason to get away from tourist corridors. Some gems stand out, like a 1950s Italian language Isaac Asimov collection, black and white promotional photos of movie actors from the 1930s, a huge collection of 45 rpm records, and detailed tomes of Renaissance art. Sadly, my budget and luggage cannot handle a spree... a perfect excuse to save each penny.

Europe is a melting pot and Rome is dubbed the eternal city, drawing visitors from across the region and around the globe. But the 20-something barista gives a narrow squint as I order espresso in English at a trendy hole-in-the-wall. Switching to French helps, but the cold glare continues. It is hard to say if pride drives this ("speak Italian!"), or a genuine disdain. They are busy. Perhaps it is tourist fatigue.

Narrow winding streets channel me to the Parthenon, where I discover a chaotic scene. The Italian economy is bad, and the regular Friday labor protest is shadowed by three dozen police dressed for a riot, paramilitary assault vehicles down each side street, and a noisy helicopter overhead. The locals turn out to enjoy the spectacle, which features crimson smoke grenades and loud chanting.

Ed has been anxious for news of his grandmother. A message awaits our return to the ship, saying she has passed. He gazes seaward and cries in silence as we sail into the Tyrrhenian Sea.

So long as the memory of certain beloved friends lives in my heart, I shall say that life is good. ˜ Helen Keller

> *If your actions inspire others to dream more, learn more, do more, and become more, you are a leader. ~ John Quincy Adams*

It is a beautiful Saturday to visit both Pisa and Florence and turn our minds from the sad news at home. My bus passes beneath ruins of other public works, arches soaring 30 meters tall, supporting an aqueduct that is still intact but serves no function other than nostalgia. The road is the width of six war horses ridden abreast. This allowed a departing army to pass another returning to Rome, each led by three mounted officers. Umbrella pines shade the ancient path, a leafy awning planted 2,000 years ago. The trees are still doing an admirable job.

Inside a walled courtyard I approach the impressive Duomo complex at Pisa, gargoyle-shaped leaden rainspouts ready but dormant. Frugal (but foolish) builders only applied roof tiles to the side facing the prevailing weather, and now the down-weather side requires much more maintenance. Foolishness continues: the famous leaning tower was planned to house clarion bells but required some... *rework*. It is now well supported, sometimes by fingers in whimsical photographs.

Florence (or Firenze) boasts museums, monuments, and leather shops around the central plaza, built from weathered copper stone. I settle into a nameless family-run trattoria off the beaten track, away from other tourists. Linguini with giant prawns in a light and garlicy red sauce, and a glass of the house white to wash down robust dark grain bread makes a relaxing lunch. Then back to the plaza.

Inside the silent Basilica of Santa Croce I inspect monuments to famous Firenzii artists and thinkers, including Guglielmo Marconi, Galileo Galilei, and Enrico Fermi. Around the corner is *Il Porcellino*, a bronze fountain of a giant boar, which inspired its twin in Sydney. Legend says a coin placed in the statue's mouth that slides immediately into the drain yields good luck. My technique is perfect and my very first Euro goes right in. I expect a handsome return from this piglet. Each bit counts and I'll take any luck I can get.

Daily Position: N 43º 46' 11", E 011º 15' 35"
Status: In Port, Livorno, Italy to visit Pisa and Firenze
Weather: perfectly clear, 27º C, NW 12 kts, 1 m waves

DAY 42

MONTE CARLO, MONACO

JUNE 30

Helicopters come and go from nearby yachts as we anchor just offshore Monaco. I get a splashy seat on a speedy launch and step ashore in the second-smallest country on earth, just two square kilometers of densely packed apartments, museums, and casinos. Perhaps I will test my luck and win some gold?

Outside the Musée Oceanographique I pose by a tiny yellow submarine, double turreted and bright. Inside the entry, sea creatures depicted in mosaic tile cover the terrazzo floor. A conch shell-themed staircase leads me down into a massive underground cavern. Aquaria, tank upon tank, fill the space: tuna and rays, sharks and coral, angelfish, clownfish, zebrafish, spiny lobster, and a brooding, doleful octopus who I dub Iago. Crab, eel, barnacle, sole, sturgeon, krill - they are all represented.

Back on the main floor, my jaw drops at a wall of irregular boxes, 15 meters high and 40 wide, a life-sized knick-knack shelf packed to overflowing with artifacts and memorabilia from Monaco's early 20th century oceanographic expeditions. Mummified seals, a towering taxidermied *ursus maritimus* and stuffed penguins hold court among hardware: diving bells, pressure suits, harpoons, life buoys, and models of ships. The hall to the left is a tribute to these expeditions, showcasing photographs and ship's log entries made by Prince Albert I himself.

Ed discovers an unattended podium and steps up to deliver yet another lecture. The ceiling is painted in ocean scenes, each framed by inlaid wood and intricate gilding. We relax for a lunch of salad, buffalo mozzarella, and espresso on a rooftop terrace draped in grape vines. The air taxi fleet does a brisk business. I fend off a persistent seagull.

A greening copper statue of Odysseus fixes me in his piercing gaze. He is visible only from the marina, for the enjoyment of those who arrive by sea. Like this famous mariner, I feel the inexorable pull to the ocean's magic and mystery. Shiny gold is nothing compared to the promise of adventure.

The sea, once it casts its spell, holds one in its net of wonder forever.
~ Jacques Cousteau

> *Only put off until tomorrow what you are willing to die having left undone. - Pablo Picasso*

Art Nouveau has always been a personal favorite, and I can't wait to get ashore in Barcelona to see premier examples of the style carried into architecture, in the whimsical buildings of the great Catalan architect Antoni Gaudi.

For the 1992 Olympics, city elders approved a nine-month plan to remove the ancient city wall, long reviled for messing up traffic and trade. Disgruntled citizens showed up the next day with picks and shovels, and cleared it in a weekend. More than 20 years later the city's facelift still feels fresh, inviting, and clean. It is fun to see their patron creature, the bat, on every lamppost.

Gaudi's work is scattered throughout the city, but is fully on display at the glorious *Parc Guell*, planned as an exclusive gated community. His serpentine bench is a prime example of organic influence realized in reclaimed tile. It is without question the most comfortable bench I have ever sat upon. The multi-colored mosaic salamander "el drac" fountain at the park entrance is completely mobbed and I can't even get close. Instead I tap my foot to the echoes of a flamenco guitar beneath vaulted pillars in the park's open-air marketplace.

La Sagrada Família is a living example of medieval cathedrals that took generations to complete. Under construction since 1882, three façades tell the story of Christ's birth, life, and death. Gaudi only saw the first façade completed, but left instructions that still guide the builders to an expected completion in 2026. All of creation is represented in the exterior statues, and the interior is a rising forest of multi-colored concrete and stone, interlinking catenaries that mirror gravity and draw my eyes toward heaven.

Ed remarks with embarrassment about his jaundiced photographer's eye, skipping great shots in search of something "better." Five ports in five days. Each monument-filled city should be granted a week, at least, but we are on a schedule and dashing around the planet.

Daily Position: N 41º 23' 17", E 002º 11' 41"
Status: In Port, Barcelona, Spain
Weather: clear blue, 23º C, NW 17 kts, 2 m waves

FRAN
Bordea
Ma
na
Barcelona
Madrid Balear
Lisbon
SPAIN Is.
Malaga
ALG
©1996

Daily Position: N 37º 01' 27" W 001º 19' 17"
Status: Southwest course to enter the Western Hemisphere
Weather: overcast, 22º C, NE 5 kts, 1 m waves

DAY 44

Through the morning we maintain a south-westerly course, passing Ibiza on our port side to round Costa Blanca on our starboard. This is the last day sailing the calm waters of the Mediterranean. In just two weeks I have met so many friendly people and have spoken their languages: Hebrew, Greek, Turkish, Italian, French, and Spanish. Connecting with each of them for a brief moment has changed their stories, and they have changed mine.

The pace has been relentless. The heat has been oppressive. The days have been exhausting. Daily travel to and from historical sites takes its toll as I fight tumor-induced motion sickness. Staying ahead of the right medication is a constant chore. Cancer tries to hold me back, but I am determined to battle forward. The rewards of discovery, learning, and exploration far outweigh the effort. Fighting hard is good. I have two more months at sea, and the rest of the world to capture.

GOLFE DU LION

The ship is closer to the Atlantic, which means better internet. We sit on deck and clink ice in tall glasses of tea. In this welcome break from exploring ashore I catch up on correspondence. Over 1,500 pictures in seven days. Some merely show the flavor of a place, but many tell stories that span thousands of years, of dreams long gone, of backbreaking work and struggle, of enduring hope for a better future. We should all try to leave a lasting mark with our daily efforts.

The funeral wake for Ed's grandmother is being held today. He is saddened by a note from home, a transcript of remarks to be made for those she left behind. Grandma was a lifelong learner and sent us off enthusiastic about this adventure, with a knowing sparkle in her eyes. We travel onward to make her proud.

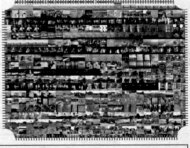

JULY 2

The sun goes and the Atlantic fog rolls in, obscuring rocky Gibraltar in a swirling gray mist. I hear sound signals on both sides. We slip the pass and exchange tranquil waters for hard ocean swells. The mist makes me shiver, and I head below for a night of fitful sleep.

In matters of style, swim with the current. In matters of principle, stand like a rock. ~ Thomas Jefferson

> *The best thing to hold onto in life is each other.*
> ~ Audrey Hepburn

Back upon the ocean once more! It smells like *home*, an invigorating "big water" smell again after the inland seas. The ship makes a leisurely approach to Cadiz, Spain's gateway to the Atlantic. Raiders came ashore here for centuries, Moorish and Phoenician and Visigoth. Today it is us.

I am headed to Seville, with no plans other than to replace small consumable items, and avoid a particularly notorious barber. Where Barcelona excelled at reusing broken ceramics, Seville elevates decorated tile to a high form of art. Whole buildings are adorned in tile. These tiles are not mere patterns placed in pleasing tessellations, but are individually painted and fired, installed to form striking murals in glaze. Each entryway begs a visit, beckoning blue and gold and spiraled iridescent, trumpeting the affluence and artistry of its residents.

First order of business: shopping. General shops are called bazaars and have a dollar store feel, aisles packed with hardware, toys, silk flowers, obsolete electronic gadgets, wrapping paper. At a grocer I ask for a quarter kilo of plums. They do not understand quarter. I type 1/4 on my cell phone and the light comes on: *cuarto*! Yes, of course. I am required to show my passport to charge seven Euros on a credit card. Our American cards are hopelessly obsolete without chips.

Finding lunch proves difficult. The first counter does not understand my pronunciation. Perhaps I lack a southwestern Spanish accent. They refuse to take my order, do not show me a seat. After staring blankly at each other I move on, still hungry. Across *El Puente de Isabelle II*, its railings festooned with lovers' locks, I wander into Taberna el Papelón, abandoned in the mid-afternoon. The ceiling tinkles with hanging green bottles. A cigarette machine in the corner offers Camels and Chesters and Lucky Strikes. Focaccia and salad arrive quickly, chased with Estrella beer. Getting off the beaten track certainly has benefits. Tourist-free, it is a heavenly meal.

Daily Position: N 37º 22' 48", W 005º 59' 33"
Status: In Port, Cadiz, Spain to visit Seville
Weather: clear sky, 27º C, light airs, harbor is calm

DAY 46

LISBON, PORTUGAL

JULY 4

Daily Position: N 38º 42' 17" W 009º 07' 41"
Status: In Port, Lisbon, Portugal, starboard-side to
Weather: clear sky, 31º C, E 9 kts, 1 m waves

The Targus River is calm under high pressure and blazing summer sun. Our ship passes under *Ponte 25 de Abril*, a suspension bridge renamed after the 1974 military revolution. Lisbon sits along an earthquake zone, and the bridge is the twin of San Francisco's Golden Gate. Engineering drives design. I take advantage of our late arrival to do laundry. Ed is on deck taking photos.

Walking ashore with no set plans, I encounter that typical den of thieves who congregate at the head of the pier, a loose confederation of taxi drivers. One approaches with a grinning licentious look that screams, "Yes I am about to overcharge you, and yes you are about to pay me." His brown Mercedes is quiet and clean. Twenty euros drops me across the street from *Padrão dos Descobrimentos*, Monument to the Discoveries. This prideful edifice is marred by graffiti, but thankfully not unchallenged; a pedestrian underpass has many spots scrubbed clean. The marble-like concrete monument jutting into the channel showcases famous Portuguese explorers like Henry the Navigator, Vasco de Gama, and Ferdinand Magellan. The plaza is a frozen ocean cast in mosaic bricks, depicting Age of Discovery tendrils stretching across the world.

Nautical artifacts, thousands, capture my imagination for the rest of the afternoon as I pick my way through the Maritime Museum's dense collection. The rapid advance in seakeeping technology is revealed by ship models, each iteration eclipsing the last in complexity and utility. Planispheric astrolabes, octants and sextants and quadrants, equatorial sundials, diptych compasses, and intricate slide rules carved from ivory are all testament to the dedicated love of adventure (and riches) shown by a great colonial power.

My return cab, a dilapidated Volvo, costs eight euros. Extreme speed and open windows must pass for air conditioning. In the distant past (a month ago) we sailed the Orient, but with cool winds on the bow, the Atlantic softly beckons.

An investment in knowledge always pays the best interest.
~ Benjamin Franklin

> *Not all those who wander are lost.*
> *~ J. R. R. Tolkien*

No question, a night spent on the open ocean makes for different sleep than on an inland sea. Swells are longer, more powerful. The ship does not roll, it surges. Imagine the difference between being nudged by a puppy and being nudged by an elephant, and you will understand a bit of what I mean. Topside the temperature is markedly cooler. We are not surrounded by islands and continents anymore and the open water is a bit scary. The indistinct horizon has returned, a blurry line where the planet drops away, the always inscrutable edge of the world.

Back to at-sea routine. Very first thing, the purser's staff drops by to collect our passports for stamping before Ireland. Ed does laundry, attends a port brief for Cobh and Dublin, helps the passenger choir with final run-throughs for tomorrow's concert, and sifts through our growing stack of ticket stubs and maps. In the afternoon I spend some time doing research based on my grandmother's maiden name. She was born in Cork, near our next port call, and would have some stories to tell. "The old country" will, for me, be something entirely new.

Down below in the engineering spaces they are working through a minor crisis: one of the reverse osmosis machines is acting up. So far this trip we have had very little rationing of water. Ed talks about his time deployed in the tropics when "the evaporator" went down, and sea showers were strictly enforced. Normally the ship has full water tanks and can pump extra fresh water production over the side. Somehow, fresh water supplies have gotten critically low.

Loud "pipes" (announcements) squawk over the speakers, for the Chief Engineer to "lay" (hurry) to a certain obscure spot "on the double" (quickly). We passengers are regularly scolded to "maintain water discipline." By mid-afternoon all systems are fixed and we breathe a sigh of relief. Not having potable water would be an embarrassment for the Engineer but a major issue for us.

Daily Position: N 42º 13' 54", W 009º 48' 47"
Status: Underway on a northerly course, making 22 kts
Weather: clear skies, 21º C, N 20 kts, 2 m waves

Daily Position: N 47º 23' 00" W 009º 07' 32"
Status: Underway in the Bay of Biscay, northerly course
Weather: Partly cloudy, 17º C, E 19 kts, 2 m waves

DAY 48

CELTIC SEA

JULY 6

Lost in thought, I watch a lone gull riding an updraft, hovering over the ship. A dip of her head and a small deflection of a wing-tip feather are all she needs to change her path, drifting across the bow and back. She sees my gaze and returns it, hoping for a treat. One of the great privileges of going to sea is watching birds in flight, suspended above and drifting like lazy, untethered kites. But unlike kites there is intelligence behind the watchful eyes, a reason for being here. Our ship is a way station, a moving island upon which to rest, before darting once more aloft to find places unknown.

Vikings were said to carry dark and hearty ravens on long voyages. When released within 200 miles of shore, the ravens would fly away and point the direction to the nearest land. If we tried that today, the raven would just circle in the stiff easterly wind, or be blown out to sea. The Bay of Biscay is to starboard, our position too far from shore.

Keeping us all distracted after yesterday's water incident seems to be the order of the day. The ship schedules a cooking demonstration mid-morning, and an egg drop contest after the noon meal; I attend the first and skip the second. The head cook is from Germany and mighty funny, playing straight man against another senior officer from India, who would do well at standup. Comedians with cleavers and toques. Ed attends a port brief about Glasgow and starts planning our excursion across Scotland.

In the afternoon I listen to the passenger choir. The show is popular with both travelers and many of the crew. I still get mistaken for crew myself, but this is mainly because I tend to get involved and lend a hand where I can. So many people seem to just wait for the next shiny object to distract them, a pre-packaged diversion created by someone else. I resolve to join the choir for their next show, which should make my *not crew* status rather obvious. Generous cacophony may result, but I will be making my own fun.

Every day is a journey, and the journey itself is home.
~ Matsuo Basho

It is Australia Day in Cobh. I am up early to watch maneuvers and docking. The local merchants have decorated their storefronts to show Aussie pride. Can you imagine a stuffed kangaroo holding a harp and dressed in a kilt? Such a lark could only happen on the Emerald Isle.

This town was the last port for HMS Titanic passengers, before a cold night filled with ice changed their lives forever. It is a tiny cramped village working uphill from a cozy wharf. A straight-ish street leads me past a neat row of houses, identical except for paint: pink, green, blue, brown. The street is silent. The residents are all in town, watching the spectacle of their little cove overrun by sailors from down under.

The hill is steep, but I continue upward, sweat building beneath my shirt in proportion to the heat of the day. I stop for breath by a pewter plaque hung to remember a local celebrity who left here aboard Titanic, which on that day was just another ship in port. I crest the hill and am happy for the flat. The single homes here are well kept. Small front gardens and cropped, dense hedges between plots speak of owners with more leisure time, or perhaps better gardeners.

A cemetery at the top of the hill spreads before me, with grandeur fit for a movie. Row upon row, line upon line of monuments and pillars, some new and crisp, others weathered and mossy. I am stunned into silence. It is the realization of time, locked in these stones. Here generation after generation lived, here they died, and left memorials to themselves on a sloping, misty plain. Stories lost in the heather.

Back in town everyone from mayor to wee babe is here to celebrate our visit, with music by the Army band, rowdy sea chantey singers, colorful vendors and speeches. I munch cheddar crisps and a honeycomb-flavored ice cream cone. Ed and I both phone our parents, send our love, and catch up on news from home. Stepping back into the street, the party is just getting started.

DAY 49

COBH, IRELAND

JULY 7

Daily Position: N 51º 51' 04", W 008º 17' 48"
Status: In Port, Cobh, Ireland for Australia Day
Weather: Partly Cloudy, 23º C, light airs, harbor calm

Daily Position: N 53º 20' 51" W 006º 12' 56"
Status: In port, Dublin, Ireland for a pint of Guinness
Weather: Sky clear, 23º C, E 7 kts, harbor calm

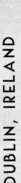

DAY 50

DUBLIN, IRELAND

JULY 8

Getting up the coast into Dublin City takes until well past breakfast. A late departure last night might have had something to do with this. We are alongside at 11:00 a.m. I step ashore with a song in my heart, to visit the famous Guinness factory for a tour and a pint.

Some landmarks are well known, others would like to be. The Brazen Head screams "Ireland's oldest pub!" but I have no way to check the claim's authenticity. The striking Samuel Beckett Bridge pays tribute to the influential avant-garde novelist with a cable-stayed spar resembling a giant harp, symbol of the nation. St. Patrick's Cathedral heard the first performance of Handel's Messiah in April of 1742. Why would the German-born composer pick here of all places for the premiere, and not Munich or Berlin? Here in the cathedral's famous shadow, the choice seems understandable. My presence brings this dusty brochure fact back to life. Presence makes history *real*.

Finally, the Guinness Storehouse at the St. James Gate Brewery is before me, an eight-story museum offered in tribute to the world's most famous creamy stout. Now, I am not a big beer fan but I do love a good pint of Guinness, and it will never taste more authentic than here at the source. Pristine water is a critical ingredient and I learn about early battles over water rights, well secured after 230 years. John Gilroy's famous advertising mascots from the 1930s are on display: seal, kangaroo, ostrich and, my favorite, the colorful and mischievous toucan.

My self-guided ticket includes a free pint, so I climb to the circular top floor, with sweeping views across the city. The bar is shaped to resemble a pint glass, patrons packing in to become the symbolic foam, a spirited mixture of languages and dress from around the world. The "black stuff" does not disappoint, famous sinking bubbles cascading down the iconic curvy glass, the dark stout slipping past my tongue with smooth and malty bliss. Urgency fades as I shout with a grin, "round two if you please, barkeep!"

The innocent and the beautiful have no enemy but time.
~ William Butler Yeats

> *I thought how unpleasant it is to be locked out; and I thought how it is worse, perhaps, to be locked in.* ~ *Virginia Woolf*

Pipers welcome us on a clear day. Puffy clouds follow along across a marshy landscape. Place names choked with history are wildly strange yet strangely perfect: Gleneagles, Fyfe, Broxton, Dogbies, Carnarvon Bar, McGrouther, and Glenbervie golf course, Scotland's most expensive.

Set amongst rocky crags and the winding river Forth, charming Stirling is one of Scotland's oldest towns, the gateway to Loch Lomond, and the crossroads between Highlands and Lowlands. Stirling Castle was besieged sixteen times during its long and bloody history, and Scottish Kings and Queens have been crowned here, including Mary, Queen of Scots in 1543. Combing quaint shops builds my appetite for lunch at Mamma's Muffins: focaccia bread, brie cheese, cranberries, and red onions, panini-pressed until just gooey. Ed excitedly enters one of his favorite backcountry outfitters, the Mountain Warehouse. We stock up on cold weather gear for the next leg of our journey across northern Europe: woven buffs, windbreakers, and woolen socks.

Later in the day I tour one of the engineering marvels of the 21st century - The Falkirk Wheel. Inaugurated in 2002 by Queen Elizabeth II, this massive revolving lock resembles a giant screw, and is the world's only rotating boat lift. A century ago, 11 locks connected Glasgow's Clyde Canal with Edinburgh's Union Canal, spanning the 79-foot difference in elevation between the canals. Now it takes just one slow turn, like a key in a lock. I board a canal boat, sail across the aqueduct and enter the tub, to be lifted into space from one waterway and gently floated into another. The upper canal enters a north-south tunnel, a hundred meters long. Three boats wait in the far basin to be lowered with me on the return trip. We all motor in, tie to platinum cleats, shut down, and enjoy the ride. Archimedes' principle ensures each side stays perfectly balanced. Nuanced and precise engineering makes for another enlightening day.

Daily Position: N 56º 03' 50", W 003º 55' 55"
Status: In Port, Greenock, Scotland, to visit the Falkirk lock
Weather: Light scattered, 24º C, NW 6 kts, harbor calm

Daily Position: N 50° 54' 30" W 006° 00' 24"
Status: Southerly courses down the Irish Sea
Weather: light scattered, 19° C, NE 8 kts, 1 m waves

Underway again, retracing the trackline south through the Irish Sea. The morning waters are calm during my brisk walk about the decks, but the wind bites. I zip tight the snug grey windbreaker I bought yesterday.

The ship passes several dome-shaped islands, granite heads of undersea giants hung about with mottled mops of green leafy scrub. The Isle of Man retreats from view, far to port. During the last ice age this entire area was a vast inland freshwater lake that slowly returned to the sea as the glaciers retreated. These little round islands were then prominent mountaintops. Now humbled by time and stubbornly empty of people, they hold my gaze in the morning mist, quiet nesting places for sea birds.

Late in the day Penwith, the southwestern peninsula of Wales, comes into view. The ship rounds the point where rocky crags make a sharp transition from angled basalt to the softer and more famous chalky cliffs. This is Land's End. What thought comes to mind when I mention Land's End? Do you think sheep and salt spray and heather, or of the iconic clothing brand? Being here links sight, sound, feel, and smell to conjured thoughts of a mythical place. The place before me is vividly real, and yet I discover at the same time that any lingering enchantment is gone. It is really just another spot on the planet, isolated and alone. Some have said you should never go back to the place you grew up, especially if you loved it. Travel, for romantics, is the ultimate spoiler, like dropping a Ming Dynasty vase or a Fabergé egg. The delicate beauty of the thing that was is lost and gone in a blink. Like growing up, ugly harsh shards of a formerly beautiful image are all that remain.

Into the western end of the narrow English Channel with the rushing current I go. The French call this water *La Manche*, the sleeve, closing in from both sides on our easterly track. Sunset strikes the less-famous but still impressive white cliffs of Normandy. Worldly fame is often just better marketing.

Failure is just life trying to move us in another direction.
~ Oprah Winfrey

> *Impossible is a word to be found only in the dictionary of fools.*
> *~ Napoleon Bonaparte*

The ship crosses *Baie de la Seine*, embarks the harbor pilot, and is fast alongside by 7:00 a.m. Half the days and half the time zones have passed beneath our keel. Many of my shipboard friends dash ashore for a tiring day in Paris, but I just want to dawdle in the country and practice my French. Honfleur, a quaint fishing village and birthplace of the Impressionist art movement, seems like just the ticket.

Tudor-style post-and-beam cottages nestle into rolling folds across the sweeping countryside, like ocean birds sheltering in dunes from a storm. Their thatched rooftops are growing and alive with moss, straw, and self-seeded wildflowers. Often a house has masonry walls, five-sided bookends of stone, filled in between with light plaster, mismatched windows, and curved beams reclaimed from a shipwright's yard. Creamy-skinned cows lounge beneath orchards of fruit ripening in the sun, apples destined to become Calvados at a local *cidrerie*.

Sailboats pack the *Vieux Bassin* with the unassuming efficiency of a harbor that has hosted working boats for 10 centuries. This city was little damaged during World War II, one of the few in Normandy to retain its old country character. Sharp flint is part of every cemented wall. Rounded cobblestones pave weathered streets. A rainbow queue of ancient brick buildings flank the quay, drunkenly leaning against each other for support. A black cat sniffs at a baby playing in the street. Morning glories crowd a window box, delicate starbursts of bright yellow and a purple so deep it looks almost black.

Shops reflect the town's ocean-going roots. A brazen three-story billboard promises to cure *mal de mer* - seasickness. At a trendy cafe in the center of town, *Le Chat Qui Peche* (the cat who fishes), I enjoy a warm pastry, moist and eggy inside a pleasingly crunchy golden crust, and wash it down with *cidre fermie de la cave*. Easy and unrushed; a fitting end for this crazy port-packed segment.

> **Daily Position:** N 49º 29' 24", E 000º 06' 00"
> **Status:** In Port, Le Havre, France, starboard-side to
> **Weather:** partly cloudy, 18º C, NE 7 kts, 1 m waves

Sailing

Segment

Three

DAY 54

From Le Havre to Dover is just over 100 nautical miles. We make the crossing at just under 10 knots and wake to see a vertical wall of white, topped by a rocky castle. Artificial seawalls define the harbor, and we moor at the western docks to avoid heavy cross-channel ferry traffic to the east.

My parents visited here in the early 1970s and still have vivid memories of cordial hospitality, bland food, and really bad coffee. Dad swam across the channel and back as part of a relay team and was later inducted into the International Swimming Hall of Fame.

This is a major swap day for the ship's crew, and a segment transfer for many passengers. It is always wise to avoid any ship's activity that does not involve you, so I board a double-decker bus (which is driven on the left, of course) headed for town.

DOVER, ENGLAND, UK

Before long I arrive at Dover Castle to a shocking fee: 15 euros. After three weeks with the currency, I grudgingly compare this to the price of a good meal. Thankfully, the castle turns out to be a robust meal for the mind. My footsteps echo in the gatehouse tunnel. An interior wall hides a secret garden, but Ed boosts me to get a view. Naughty. In the main castle, detailed exhibits are scripted for children in both French and English. Every cemented stone is set about by flint, neatly stacked on the diagonal, row upon row. In the keep's main kitchens, period cookware is on display. This may be my dream kitchen. Oh, what feasts I could prepare in here! The upper floors show how the nobles and their families lived, surrounded by red velvet tapestries and sturdy tables covered in linen. But the windowless stone walls, vital for military protection, radiate darkness and cold.

JULY 12

Stormy clouds gather over the channel. The full ship's company completes emergency drills. While donning life vests, we happen upon newly arrived sailors Merrilyn and John, who hosted us in Sydney two months ago. Serendipity has brought us together again.

We wander for distraction, but we travel for fulfillment.
~ Hilaire Belloc

> *A mind stretched by a new idea never goes back
> to its original dimensions. ~ Oliver Wendel Holmes, Sr.*

5 ♠

England is closer to the Netherlands than it is to Ireland or Scotland...at least by straight-line distance. Little wonder the place is a bizarre but still vibrant mish-mash of Anglo, Norse, and Continental language, art, and architecture. Many examples of modern sculpture are on public display: a giant striped floating duck; a pink-shirted man with red wooden shoes and a giant green apple for a head; a truncated platinum plinth, oval in cross-section and stamped through with a hole.

My first stop is a restored iconic windmill, now a private residence. They must just love the daily parade of tourists (like me) snapping photos in their front yard. At a busy barge stop under a canopy of willows draping to the water, I board a launch, propelled by eco-friendly natural gas. The canals are laid out like roads, sweeping rings over-girded by lift bridges for bicycles and feet. I float past the Anne Frank *Huis*, the Tulip Museum, a three-masted barque *Amsterdam*, and a happy family piloting their custom barge - a giant wooden keg of Heineken. Crenelated brick buildings with variegated decorations line both sides of the canal, each with a rooftop spar for lifting materials from below.

Once again on the street, I drop into a basement crêperie, bragging the best crêpes in Amsterdam. The specialty of the house is *au Grand Marnier*, but they also offer ham and cheese, spinach and feta, and Nutella selections. Then, shopping for supplies, I am embarrassed again by my antiquated U. S. credit card - no chip means no sale. Ed's splitting headache means he can't focus, so I take charge, withdraw cash from a bank machine, and pay with euros.

After some perfectly drawn espresso at The Otherside coffeeshop, a marijuana bar just off Kerkstraat, I finish the afternoon in the tulip market. Also on this corner: the Torture Museum and Medieval Exhibition, and Bubbles Erotic Café. Thanks for inviting my business, truly, but it is time to be moving on.

Daily Position: N 51º 55' 00", E 004º 30' 00"
Status: In Port, Rotterdam, Netherlands
Weather: Light scattered, 22º C, light airs, harbor calm

Daily Position: N 56º 14' 36" E 007º 02' 12"
Status: North-northeasterly courses through the North Sea
Weather: mostly cloudy, 16º C, W 31 kts, 3 m waves

DAY 56

NORTH SEA

JULY 14

Northeast we go, a 23-hour day to make the time zone happy, into the Skagerrak to escape the North Sea. The ship's bow pounds a path through stacked, steep waves all night, sending shivers up and down the steel frames, vibrating overhead panels and bulkheads. The shifting wind is to blame, a change from days of warm easterly breezes. Now a strong west wind drives water landward to fetch against Jutland. Wavelets build into monsters.

Ed tells a story of sailing these waters aboard the three-masted tall ship EAGLE in 1989, on the way to a port call at Leningrad, USSR. Tensions were high. The Cold War was at an end, but the crew had been briefed to be on the lookout for any actionable intelligence. A regular tradition was to man the yardarms, one sailor standing at the end of each yard, clutching a cable for support. Assigned to the foremast and the highest 'royal' yard, Ed had a great view of the Soviet port below. Upon arrival, tugboats jockeyed for 'first touch' and one impacted the port side. The shock vibrated to the top of the masts, almost knocking several sailors off their feet. Loud curses came down from the conning officer, the tugs backed off, and EAGLE finished mooring on her own.

Up and about late, I head straight to lunch: curried fish, garden salad, and pasta with light onion dressing. On the way back to the cabin I attend a cruise critic meeting, hosted by experts in travel by sea. They form a powerful union and are viewed warily by the ship's crew. With nothing else scheduled, the afternoon is perfect for reading and a short nap to make up last night's missing hour. The ship rounds Grenen and leaves the North Sea behind. The angry waves die down, sunshine returns, the clouds lift. But the sea is still dark and streaked with foam.

At dinner the dress is formal. Ed wolfs down an ice cream sundae decorated like a volcano. Before nightfall, Norway is far astern, Sweden to port, and Denmark is there before us, fine on the starboard bow.

Home Is Where Your Heart Is
(Backer Patrick "Pady" Morf)

74

> *You can design and create and build the most wonderful place in the world. But it takes people to make the dream a reality. ~ Walt Disney*

The harbor pilot is aboard at 5:45 a.m. to guide us through the narrow strait between Denmark and Sweden, safely threading the breakwater to find our berth.

The words "let me tell you a story" have been described as the six most seductive words in the English language. This is the hometown of Hans Christian Anderson, a famous teller of tales, immortalized here with a bronze statue. Legend says, "touch the brim of his hat, and become a gifted storyteller." So that statue becomes my quest. But first, I step ashore to visit another statue, a tribute to his story "The Little Mermaid." Her body and feet face the land, her new home, but she looks fondly, mournfully, over her right shoulder at the sea she left behind. Isn't this just the story of youth? Getting older, it is easier for me to see that greener grass truly exists on both sides of the beach. The contrast is what makes life beautiful.

Later in the day I visit Tivoli, an amusement park smack dab in the heart of the city. Another famous storyteller visited this place, not once but three times in the 1940s, gathering ideas for his first magical theme park in Anaheim. A familiar formula is at work here, but after so much time it is hard to tell whether Tivoli is the original or has been inspired in turn by the success of Disneyland. Miles of walking tends to build an appetite, satisfied in a relaxing black-and-white bistro, with macarons, rum cake, and a robust and frothy café latté.

Wind-blown grit chases my dusty footsteps back to Nyhavn. Sharp townhouses in gray-blue, burnt yellow, and brick red hues guard the waterfront. I linger in a glassblower's shop, colored swirls frozen and sparkling in the afternoon sun. I lament my transient status and the very real curse of small ships and suitcases: no room for shopping.

The ship thrusts off the berth, retraces her courses, disembarks the pilot, and continues north up Kattegat. Yet again, the trackline trends in the 'proper' direction - west.

Daily Position: N 55° 40' 34", E 012° 34' 06"
Status: In Port, Copenhagen, Denmark
Weather: overcast, 18° C, NW 11 kts, 1 m waves

Daily Position: N 59º 52' 20" E 010º 43' 06"
Status: In Port, Oslo, Norway, port-side-to
Weather: high overcast, 18º C, N 8 kts, fjord calm waters

DAY 58

OSLO, NORWAY

JULY 16

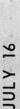

ailing into the port of Oslo reminds me of sailing around Penobscot Bay in Maine, with the smooth gray rocks coming down to the shore and the not-quite-ocean smell of coastal kelp, mixed with pine forest growing on the rolling post-glacial hills. Tiny islands, mere rocks in the fjord, have here been marked by mariners for centuries, first with whitewashed wooden towers and now by towers of steel, topped by solar panels and beacons of electric light.

Another passenger says "This place looks just like a typical Norwegian village." It would be quite hard for the village to look any different, I suspect. One small island at the north end of Oslofjord looks to be an exclusive community. Every house is painted either yellow or red, except for two jokers who flout convention and have painted theirs blue. We moor port-side-to next to Akershus Castle, copied by Disney for EPCOT, a fortress frequently besieged but never breached.

fter lunch I take the harbor ferry to visit the world's best-preserved wooden Viking funereal ships, excavated to reveal 9th century implements, tools, harnesses, textiles, and household utensils from the Oslo Fjord tombs at Gokstad, Oseberg, and Tune. Archaeologists have reproduced accurate scale models of these ships, to check stability and sea-keeping qualities using modern tow-tank analysis. The verdict: the Vikings knew what they were doing. Many of the fabrics preserved in the mounds are thought to have come from Turkey and Greece.

A brisk downhill walk brings me to the *Norsk Maritimt Museum* and the research ship FRAM, made famous by expeditions to both polar regions. Ed poses with a portrait of a childhood hero, Roald Amundsen, who led the first successful trek to the South Pole. Ed reverently touches the handle to the captain's stateroom. The great explorer himself turned it each night before retiring, weary after long days of research and discovery.

Daylight lingers, and tonight the sun stubbornly refuses to set.

5♣

There is no bad weather, only bad clothing. ~ *Norwegian Proverb*
Adventure is just bad planning. ~ *Roald Amundsen*

We think what you are doing is amazing. We wish you all the best and smooth sailing! (Backers Mark & Elizabeth Markley)

4♣

orns sound in the fog through the night. The wavering, regular, and sleep-depriving blasts are annoying, but are a necessary collateral of safe navigation, nonetheless. We skirt the Arctic Circle, just a few hundred nautical miles from the line where daylight and darkness trade places for half the year. The high atmospheric pressure expected at these high latitudes normally dampens the waves, but the west wind is back, raising a light chop on a pallid and brumey sea.

The first event of the day is a short port brief for Torshavn, then choir practice. The ladies in my section span the range of talent, but all are in it for fun and laughs. The Captain pipes noon reports. He is worried about the weather and a nasty front approaching from the Atlantic. Past the British Isles, there is nothing left to shield us.

ow to the horizon, the geosynchronous satellites which carry our ship-to-shore communications are practically out of view. Signals are blocked by the belly of the planet and for the next two days we will roam across its brow. Sometimes at high latitudes the antenna just can't keep up with the roll; the signal must pass through many layers of atmosphere, and at low angles the ship's superstructure, stacks, and masts all get in the way. Radio silence, enforced by orbital mechanics.

The Arctic Ocean may one day become an important trade route as commercial vessels begin regular transit through the Northwest Passage. Rolling waves replace whitecaps. We steam above the 60th parallel and cross the Prime Meridian to enter the Norwegian Sea.

The day stretches to almost 21 hours. Sunlight pierces the dense cloud to illuminate tiny wavelets, flashing through the ever-present mist like droplets on a mirror. Reflected colors become muted. Our ship cuts across a black and white photograph where we make an invasive and garish splash of color. Incredibly near, a horn sounds from a phantom vessel, slipping by unseen in the fog.

DAY 59

NORWEGIAN SEA

JULY 17

Daily Position: N 58º 49' 54", E 002º 14' 24"
Status: Northwesterly courses through the Shetland Islands
Weather: Partly cloudy, 16º C, W 14 kts, 2 m waves

> Daily Position: N 61º 24' 02" W 008º 34' 18"
> Status: North Atlantic Ocean making 18 kts
> Weather: overcast, thick fog, 11º C, SW 27 kts, 3 m waves

At 3:00 a.m., I am jangled awake by the screech of metal, a rhythmic clanking that rattles the bulkheads. The ship has dropped anchor just southeast of the snug harbor of Tórshavn. Then all is quiet for two hours and I drift back to sleep, to be re-awoken by straining machinery and a squeaky capstan weighing anchor. Immediately, the hooked chunk of steel is let go again, and again hoisted aboard. But this time the engines growl fully to life, the ship swings a wide turn to port, and then south, away from land.

The ship channel here is only 100 meters wide and with 35 knots of wind on the beam, an approach to the pier is just not possible. Another key consideration when entering a harbor is the forecast weather at the time of *departure*. We might have made a successful mooring, but with freshening wind and a worsening forecast, to linger makes no sense. We would be trapped. The Captain decides to leave this - the final outpost before the deep blue - and begin our transatlantic leg a few hours early.

So we bypass the Faroes. The place is serenely beautiful, a gem in the mist. The village reminds Ed of working towns along the Alaskan coastline - Nome and Barrow and Dutch Harbor, cozy buildings tightly packed against the harsh cold, here on the fringe of the world. Over an isolated and rocky cliff, the runoff from a softening snowpack cascades down, scouring glacial boulders into the sea. The roar of the water is only imagined: I hear nothing but the howling wind.

Fog at high latitudes is ever present in the summer months, soft, white, and glowing. It obscures everything with a blanket of moisture that does not drench - it soaks. A line of tundra-covered islands disappears in our wake as the swirling marine layer descends, swallowing each dark green outcrop in turn. The fog closes in on a speck of the planet I will now probably never visit. One day to either side and my story of this place would have been quite different. Soggy with regret I head below - the fog signals are back.

Facts do not cease to exist because they are ignored.
~ Aldous Huxley

> *Stop worrying about the potholes in the road and celebrate the journey.*
> *~ Fitzhugh Mullan*

10 ♠

Through the night, weather conditions do not improve. Despite seas on the beam, the ship rode fairly well, and sleep was surprisingly easy. But by late morning the swells have really picked up. Salt spray sprinkles through the sky, blasted aloft by the ship's plunging movement through the roiling and angry North Atlantic. Wave crests blown clear, an indistinct horizon, water the color of gunmetal, a charged hint of ozone in the air - all signs of riding into the thick of a storm.

So of course I must take a bold jaunt about the weather decks. The crew has blocked off the doors to the leeward (dry) side but those on the windward (wet) side remain unlocked. I am not sure of their reasoning, as the windward side seems dangerous, much more so. My jaunt becomes a stumble. The adage is "one hand for yourself, one hand for the ship." Watching the waves, hearing the pounding surf, and trying to stay upright is an adventuresome way to pass the morning.

Like trying to photograph a rainbow, getting a good picture of waves at sea is a real challenge. The biggest culprit on days like this is salt spray on the lens. Regular wipes with a soft tissue. Step to the rail. Snap! By shooting directly off the beam, on a 90° relative bearing, my hands and body shield the lens from wayward droplets. A tripod is useless. The ship moves, the ocean moves, my hands move. Miss the shot? Just wait for the next wave. Waves come in sets of threes with a lull between. Ed once took advantage of this phenomenon while landing a helicopter on a tiny pitching deck. Watch the swells, pick your wave, and commit. Catching an egg on a plate.

Two months at sea has conditioned me to the regular movement of the decks. Discovering small bruises from a bashed shin or bumped elbow is nothing new. The best idea on a day like this, however, is to keep to the cabin, find a deep, heavy chair near a porthole, and just watch the salt spray attack the gunwales.

Daily Position: N 57º 08' 24", W 019º 25' 26"
Status: Southwesterly course across the North Atlantic
Weather: overcast, 15º C, SE 32 kts, 7 m waves

Daily Position: N 51º 17' 12" W 032º 25' 02"
Status: North Atlantic Ocean making 21 kts
Weather: overcast, 14º C, SE 33 kts, 8 m waves

Yesterday's sea state was nothing compared to this worsening onslaught of water. Every fourth roll brings a two-fisted punch, a titanic blow that 'shivers the timbers.' The wide Atlantic Ocean is named for the mythical Greek titan Atlas. The "Sea of Atlas" lives up to its mighty name. Stumbling around, fighting to stay upright with every surge and step, I feel his undeniable power.

Low atmospheric pressure all day, a deep low pressure that makes my head pound. There is a cavity in my cranium, the empty spot where the tumor was mostly (but not completely) excised by two surgeries. The space is filled with fluid, and pressure changes cause unwelcome symptoms. The headache lasts most of the day. I am not the only passenger ill at ease. The ship hangs motion sickness bags throughout the common spaces and in the ladder wells, a sure sign of rough conditions.

The track line continues on a southwesterly course, directly into the Gulf Stream, and cuts a right angle to the wind and waves. A steadier heading might be found, but courses are proscribed by the ship's navigator, well in advance of any future bad weather. The main duty of the Officer of the Watch is to faithfully follow these track lines. And so, climbing mountains of endless water, we pitch and roll across the chart.

A chart is a map of the ocean surface, showing coastlines, rocks, buoys, lighthouses and prominent features such as depth of water and aids to navigation. Sea Princess boasts over 700 paper charts, enough to cover our entire float plan: all the regions of the world. Mercator charts show a rhumb line course as a straight line, and great circles show straight on the gnomonic charts. The bridge team uses these theoretical straight lines, but today they fight along a wavering and ragged track in the general direction of North America.

Dinner is a German buffet, complete with a beer stein ice sculpture and a roast suckling pig, golden brown. All these tasteful diversions keep my attention from the worsening weather.

Wishing Michelle and Ed many more happy adventures.
(Backer Shawn Simms, SS FRG ATGT)

> *I must go down to the seas again, to the lonely sea and the sky...*
> *~ John Masefield (Backer Father Thomas Weise GGA '92)*

7 ♠

Every minute carries us from land. The ship is farther at sea than she has been at any time during the voyage. The southwesterly track line parallels that of transatlantic steamers from the last century, avoiding icebergs calving from Greenland glaciers. Isolated and alone, our best hope for survival in an emergency - from captain to the lowest deck hand - comes from right here aboard. We are all in the same boat.

It would be a mistake to think our mutual dependence means we all have the "run of the ship," however - far from it. We passengers are confined to the topside decks and the "hotel" spaces: commons, dining, recreation, and lodging. Food service crew can access the kitchens; engineers haunt all the grimy places in the depths; and bridge crew members work the very highest decks. Only the captain can go everywhere, and for this reason we rarely see him. But knowing we *could* see him anytime, anywhere, keeps us all on best behavior.

It is a busy day at sea. I host a mobile computing seminar at 10:00 a.m., jockey for a spot in the laundry, then, hungry as a yak, skip choir practice to gobble a hearty brunch: omelet, toast, fruit salad, and a large hot tea. My neck and shoulders are stiff after two stormy days, and while the front has passed, the ocean is more confused, disorganized and spiky. Waves no longer pummel the hull; they prickle and spritz. By mid-afternoon, the temperature has risen and the fog backs away. Visibility improves until, under a roiling and oppressive gray overcast, I can see clear to the horizon. Sun and blue pierce the unruly clouds through fleeting and ragged rents in the brume.

The choir stages a flash mob tribute to our musical directors. The surprise is total and for those lucky to be present the event becomes a lasting memory. The evening meal is curry and deep-fried comfort food. Night falls, the temperature drops, and the caterwauling horn is again unmistakable: the fog has returned.

> **Daily Position:** N 46º 35' 54", W 041º 40' 13"
> **Status:** Underway, North Atlantic Ocean
> **Weather:** overcast, 14º C, W 15 kts, 5 m waves

Daily Position: N 41º 38' 54" W 050º 16' 48"
Status: North Atlantic Ocean making 20 kts
Weather: overcast & fog, 21º C, light airs, 3 m waves

DAY 64

Iceberg- and incident-free though the night, but that blasted horn just blew and blew. HONK! Will the fog ever go away? Life inside a cloud is a lot less romantic after a few days, much less an entire week. The trackline brings us closer to the HONK! east coast of Newfoundland hour upon hour, and will turn west-southwest later in the day to cross the Grand Banks.

Long tradition sets the precedent for a regular routine aboard ship. Clocks are HONK! everywhere. The regular routine cannot be ignored. Beneath the tight schedule is the real secret, the *reason* for regular routine: regular routine lets everyone notice anything that deviates HONK! from the *normal*. Check, move on, circle back and check again. Something that was correct a minute ago can end up broken a minute later, and the sea comes in and sinks you. We passengers are in regular HONK! places during meal time, for example, which lets the crew do regular things where we are *not*. The routine never adjusts to you - so if you force a change in routine, something is gravely wrong.

NORTH ATLANTIC OCEAN

Around the time of noon bells HONK! we are within 14 nautical miles of the site where RMS Titanic sank in 1912. The Captain announces the fact. I find myself at the port rail looking out, and then chuckle at my folly. Unlike a memorial point on land, all I see here is HONK! more foggy water. The significance of the place must be conjured in my mind. Those folks were just like us, heading to the new world, on a well-worn transportation route, three days HONK! from New York and thinking about family and friends, starting to repack trunks and baggage, swapping addresses, and watching the fog. And then HONK! things got crazy and cold in the darkness as cries for help went unanswered and hope faded and then disappeared completely beneath the waves.

JULY 22

Regular routine carries me through the rest of the afternoon. Could rising temperatures mean the end of these HONK! obnoxious sound signals?

10

The key to hope is that, in every situation, you must have at least two alternatives. ~ Richard N. Bolles

> *The world is round and the place which may seem like the end may also be only the beginning.* ~ Ivy Baker Priest (Backers Linda and Floyd Palmer)

Keeping busy has become a tedious challenge. My friends and I jest with glee, "what ever shall we do today?" and answer, truthfully, with the happy retort, "why, the very same thing as yesterday, thank you very much!" We smile broadly and laugh at our wittiness. We are stuck.

The daily riddle is published. We guess the answer (surname), then fan out across the ship to locate the passenger liaison. The first to find him with the correct answer is given a bottle of champagne, and we are vying with at least one other organized group for the prize. My tablemate Roger is successful, ensuring another night of cheap bubbly for us. Quest complete, we all return to the central passenger lounge to catch up on news and shipboard rumors over coffee.

Rumors run rampant within the confines of this novelty-free, floating prison, often driven by cultural differences. We are sailing with mostly Aussies, some Kiwis, a few Brits, and a handful of us Yanks. The bridge team is mostly from the UK. The hospitality staff comes from Eastern Europe and the Philippines. Engineers are Scottish and German. Rounding out the crew, the services team is a mixed bag: Mexico, USA, South Africa. We mix well and make a lively bunch.

Gone is the fog, and with it that infernal honking horn. We have made hardly any southing, but it is warmer. Everyone bubbles topside to enjoy the sun, crew and passengers all. The ship offers a wine tasting, five vintages from around the world plus cheese, crackers, and fruit. Except for the sunshine, wine, and a lost gold hoop earring (relocated after dinner), a repeat of daily events proves inevitable, with minor variations. Cycle two loads of wash and dry through the laundry. Choir practice at noon. A change: sushi buffet for lunch. Teach a class. Walk the weather decks. Dress for dinner. Evening comedy show and trivia contest over drinks. Find my rack, turn in. Expect to do it all over again in the morning.

LATE HARVEST

Sauvignon Blanc

Daily Position: N 41º 21' 06", W 059º 44' 36"
Status: Westerly course, approaching North America
Weather: overcast, 26º C, SSW 39 kts, 4 m waves

DAY 66

NORTH ATLANTIC OCEAN

JULY 24

D riving across the Atlantic Ocean, the prevailing westerlies bring land smells from North America a full day before the watch above calls "land ho!" I have now been at sea for over two months, and the sounds and smells of the ship are completely routine and therefore unremarkable; so too the bland and unaccented smell of ocean, salt spray and moisture. My senses have been heightened by the blandness, able to detect small changes from a mundane and daily *normal*. Earthiness, airborne dust, and hints of smoke drift eastward and I can smell them. A whole continent is just *over there*.

Immigrants in the last wave of the European diaspora certainly felt the same keen anticipation as they approached New York harbor, one hundred years ago. Back then, a crossing by steam took between nine and fifteen days. Most made the voyage berthed in steerage, a miserable experience. The storms of this past week have left some present-day passengers a bit green around the gills too, despite relatively luxurious modern accommodations. Eight days at sea, and I yearn for the land.

E d and I love sailing into New York Harbor. We met here, and during college I worked in Tower One of the World Trade Center. For me, coming here is coming home. Tomorrow I will be back, and I can't wait. I am not alone in these thoughts. Excitement is building throughout the ship, and the passageways are filled with suitcases. Everyone is up early. Coffee in hand, our regular "breakfast club" members discuss the daily riddle: "The ruler of shovels, with a double, as thin as a knife, with a wife." Possible answers are all over the map.

Honoring a longtime transatlantic tradition, the passengers stage an afternoon talent show for the crew. I sing with the choir, performing "An American Trilogy," and as a service veteran, Ed helps fold a giant U. S. flag.

Following dinner the galley team treats us to another extravagant end-segment tradition: a massive pastry buffet and Baked Alaska for dessert.

...To boldly go where no one has gone before!
(Backer John "Big Z" Zeno)

Sailing
Segment
Four

> One of the greatest travel pleasures is not going to a new place,
> but traveling deeper into a familiar one. ~ Rolf Potts

Tides and harbor traffic require an early arrival. I am up before the sun to face a brisk north-westerly wind, belying the calendar's midsummer date. A near-full moon still hangs in the sky. And then I see it: the Verrazano Narrows spanned by an impressive multi-level bridge. With a sudden inhale the fog uncovers dozens of cargo ships at anchor on the western edge of upper New York harbor. The city itself appears through the same mist. Our approach makes the skyscrapers seem to rise from the water, pushed upward by sheer willpower, ambition, energy, and money. New York City has been called "the capital of the world"; the shimmering skyline this morning is worthy of the title.

Although I was among the first up, the decks are now filled with sightseers. Most lean out and strain forward, striving to be first to sight the Statue of Liberty. "There she is!" cries one excited teen-age girl, and she is right. The statue grows larger and more distinct, framed against taller but less glamorous buildings along the Hudson River's west bank. A brilliant yellow morning sun slips between the horizon and the cloud for a moment and catches the gold-leafed torch, held aloft in Lady Liberty's right hand.

A wave of excitement, an eerie feeling of shared history and pride sweeps over me. Several of my own ancestors experienced this very sight, shortly before immigration processing at Ellis Island - now a museum - a reminder of a dynamic time of change, hardship and op-portunity. I hope the United States, represented by this iconic copper colossus, can remain a beacon of freedom for the people of the world.

After a frustrating wait to clear customs, my parents meet me on the pier. I spend the short, exciting visit telling stories and hearing news from home. I leave behind purchases and take aboard supplies, enough to complete the trip. Away into the river and heading south, New York's silvery cliffs drop back into the sea.

Daily Position: N 40º 42' 46", W 074º 00' 21"
Status: In Port, New York City, USA
Weather: high overcast, 19º C, NW 10 kts, 1 m waves

Daily Position: N 36º 03' 02" W 072º 24' 48"
Status: Southerly courses in the Atlantic Ocean
Weather: Mostly sunny, 28º C, NW 5 kts, 2 m waves

DAY 68

ATLANTIC OCEAN

JULY 26

B efore dawn we are into the Gulf Stream and moving fast, on a south-southeasterly course across the North Atlantic Basin. Hurricane Dorian is swirling in the eastern Caribbean. We must decide mid-morning whether to adjust our float plan to avoid the storm, and if we do, where to go instead.

The day in New York City was a little too much and my body tells me about it today. My head is pounding after all of yesterday's activity: the early morning, many hours getting through customs and immigration, then hot July weather and the bustling crowds of people. It was great to see family and lighten the load of trinkets. My mobile phone was back on the network after months without coverage, so I made a few calls to get caught up with friends. All that, capped off by an afternoon standing at the port rail as we left for sea, watching the Freedom Tower under construction and thinking about the disaster there, really took an emotional toll. New York was where I left to meet the ship in May, so technically I have come all the way around the world, but the journey continues on. The goal remains: circumnavigate the planet by ship. There are still 137 lines of longitude to cross.

A fternoon stretches into evening. The sun dips toward the horizon, and our new captain, who took command yesterday for the remainder of the trip, finally announces his decision about Dorian: we will evade the hurricane by skipping the scheduled port stop at Antigua, and set course for Aruba. With an early change, we can run west of the forecast track and keep the storm far to port.

At the evening meal our tablemates grumble at the shift. They have all visited the new island destination before. Ed tells of three days stranded there during one of his assignments. We are running away from a hurricane, a novel notion that keeps the conversation lively. The curved outer bands reflect back pink and amber; a sparkling sunset before the storm.

10

You never lose by loving. You always lose by holding back.
~ Barbara DeAngelis

> *Be not afraid of going slowly, be afraid only of standing still.*
> ~ Chinese Proverb

2

Out of sight of land all day, we stay east of the western Atlantic current. This course means an extra 100 nautical miles before midnight, and every knot of speed opens the distance from hurricane Dorian. Our next landmark will be the Windward Passage between Cuba and Haiti.

This leg brings many changes, not just a new captain. A sizable number of passengers have come aboard for this leg only, to experience a Panama Canal transit. The newbies bring fresh energy - a short-timer's attitude - seeking a quick escape and a quick return to their lives. We, who are settled in after months aboard, are justifiably ruffled at their brash assault upon established norms. This ship has a culture, one stalwartly southern hemisphere. We walk on the left, thank you very much. We restrict our loud social voices to loud social spaces, not the corridors at three in the morning. And formal night means just that. You are expected to dress for dinner. A polo shirt has buttons, but it is not considered formal dress. Anywhere.

Irrespective of these and other norms, soundly ignored by the invading American hordes, other patterns are emerging, and not all are good. Principal among these are the rerun meals. Our galley crew makes an admirable effort to vary the daily fare, but there are only so many ways to prepare a dish of surf, turf, or fowl before the recipes come around again. Thankfully tonight brings an unexpected addition to the menu: crab meat quiche with spicy tomato sauce.

After supper, we regulars battle the new chums through the corridors for a seat in the lounge, to watch a show given by performers who joined us in New York: Motown Gold. It is good we rushed: Ed and I settle into the very last two seats, in the very front row. After the show my friends hold seats for our regular trivia game, and a solo comedy and juggling act finishes the night with humor. Hordes of rowdy landlubbers will not dampen my spirits.

Daily Position: N 29º 10' 06", W 072º 20' 36"
Status: Course due south toward the Caribbean Sea
Weather: Mostly cloudy, 28º C, SE 21 kts, 3 m waves

Daily Position: N 22º 12' 02" W 073º 23' 42"
Status: Atlantic Ocean making 21 kts
Weather: Scattered light clouds, 30º C, E 24 kts, 3 m swells

Under towering cumulus we transit Mayaguana passage to sail further south and back into the tropics. The water has been transformed into Caribbean blue, that of rare sapphire or the eyes of a Himalayan cat. The blue is deep and warm and pure, and surrounds us everywhere except in our churning wake.

DAY 70

Today I help teach a class on the upper weather deck - juggling for beginners. And of course, the first day back in the tropics comes with a typical mid-afternoon rain squall. Right over the ship. These rains are beneficial in some ways, a labor-free freshwater wash down topside. Unfortunately, I am topside with the entire class. We race inboard to complete the lesson, but not before getting drenched. Fuzzy green tennis balls bounce through the passageways and down, down, down the ladder wells. Then it is back to the cabin for a change of clothes.

ATLANTIC OCEAN

Having hosted several classes about using mobile devices, Ed and I have become the tech gurus. As I move about the ship, fellow passengers approach me often, seemingly around every turn. I want to be helpful, but it is a case of "be careful what you wish for." Once you step into the spotlight, it is difficult to switch it off. They chase me down all afternoon, trying to connect satellite internet or check their email. I retreat to my cabin and prepare for the evening meal: a thick, flavorful white seafood chowder, and corn fritters with a side of pepper sauce.

Off to starboard, a forbidden island rises dark and featureless from the sea. A forty-year embargo remains in effect for those of us holding a U. S. passport. The political winds have shifted, but the sails of statecraft remain untrimmed. It would be interesting to visit, if the float plan included a stop, but tonight I am inclined to stay aboard. The sun is about to set and I walk forward along a sheltered weather deck. The sea is alive - frothy - with flying fish. Others step topside to see Haiti and Cuba, but stop and stare in amazed silence as silver fins flash in the fading summer light.

JULY 28

7

Practice does not make perfect. Perfect practice makes perfect.
~ Vince Lombardi

DAY 71

Lazy and hazy, a mottled sun peeks above the horizon, ambered in a dusty orange haze. The swirling hurricane is well northward, and we have escaped into the Caribbean Sea. To the southeast are the Dutch Antilles and the island of Aruba, our next port of call.

It is windy and hot, and my ship and its company have settled back into a relaxed at-sea routine. A walk about the decks, then coffee and breakfast, then track down the crewman with a riddle answer (cheap champagne on the line), then cleanups and laundry. A mid-morning briefing about the upcoming port call at Curaçao in two days' time, then the noon meal, siesta, and a technology class. I help some new friends Cheryl and Ross with their laptop and their photo library. We met half a world away in India, and it is comforting to have them still along to share memories and photographs.

CARIBBEAN SEA

All day the flying fish follow, skipping across wave tops with a freshening wind on their tails. When the wind shifts counter-clockwise it is called "backing." If the wind blows in one direction for days and then backs quickly, as it does by late afternoon, the seas turn choppy and the wave crests are sheared into foam. The fish get harder and harder to see, and finally they are gone. The high heat, humidity, and spray make for a different smell than the cold northern ocean of last week; a smell more seaweedy, pungent, and organic. Dense. Mysterious. Perhaps a bit sinister, if smells can convey such a sentiment. Elusive, primal warnings are carried on the air. Serpents and whirlpools and the deep dark, lurking close by. I retreat inboard to the comforting safety of routine.

JULY 29

Conversation at the evening meal is all about plans for tomorrow, when we will visit a small desert island, the northern outpost of South America. Marionettes, handled masterfully by fellow passenger Huber, amuse before sleep finally whisks me away.

Daily Position: N 15º 58' 18", W 072º 52' 24"
Status: Caribbean Sea south of Cuba
Weather: Scattered clouds, 29º C, NE 28 kts, 1 m chop

DAY 72

ORANJESTAD, ARUBA

JULY 30

The center of Oranjestad is under construction. New and beautifully clean cars evade potholes with practiced care. The streets themselves are choked with dusty grit, not all of it the native blowing sand. Shops sit empty behind glitzy fronts, and the cross-town trolley is an incomplete track down main street. Tourist money fuels a vision that is not yet reality. I saunter past a typical front yard: dirt, weeds, a scraggly cactus or two, and a late-model jeep painted to match the orange tag, proclaiming "One Happy Island!"

Inside a fort dedicated to Willem III, an extensive archaeological museum showcases the history of these *Islas Inútiles*, the useless islands. This designation by Spanish treasure-hunters in 1515 led to complete deportation of the locals, forever linking Aruba to the slave trade. The exhibits connect the population of today to their Caquetio forebears with the theme "Many Faces, One Nation." Recent studies have revealed a native mix of 40% European, 20% African, and 40% Amerindian heritage. The pride behind an imported identity goes beyond the people: Aruba is known for their production of aloe even though the plant is not native, having been introduced from Africa. Excavations have uncovered pottery shards and beads from Columbia, the Amazon basin, North America, Africa, and Europe. Aruba, then as now, was a global crossroads, a stopover on the route to everywhere else.

Outside in the courtyard, the museum staff are preparing for this evening's music festival. I am sad that I must miss it. The music and dance will probably be just as vibrant as the swirling crosstalk of artifacts unearthed across five centuries. A local and a tourist may share the same day, but for each the day is different. My role changes my perspective. Do they envy me, as I re-board my ship? Or is it pity in their eyes, a knowing gaze reaching back half a millennium, to waves of transients from four continents? "Sail onward, traveler, and this happy island will await your return."

Never interrupt someone doing what you said couldn't be done.
~ Amelia Earhart

> To travel is to discover that everyone is wrong about other countries.
> ~ Aldous Huxley

6

Careful backtracking through the night at slow speed, first southerly and then east, brings us to Curaçao. We embark our pilot at 6:00 a.m. to assist with maneuvers toward the quay. The remnants of tropical storm Dorian have kicked the easterly trade wind into high gear, and the sky is unsettled as we approach Willemstad. At this, the largest of the "ABC Islands," the locals are on hand to greet our arrival with dance, adorned in flowing lacy dresses of crimson and royal purple.

Chalky lizards bask in the sun, but wisely swing their hind feet away from the roasting pavement and onto their backs. A local Coast Guard helicopter circles above as I walk to the famous Queen Emma pontoon bridge guarding St. Anna Bay. The bridgemaster "drives" the pivoting bridge open and shut using twin diesel outboards.

I cross the bridge and pass candy-colored Dutch-style apartments to visit the Punda quarter, and browse the colorful fronts of a local floating market. Here, Venezuelan boats arrive from the South American mainland every morning with produce and trade goods. Vendors beckon locals and tourists alike with wide grins and a hearty "bon bini!" They urge plantains and mangoes upon us, and offer progressively lower prices as we elbow past along the narrow and crowded sidewalk. Deeper into the Punda, tiny shops stock last years' fashions and gadgets. Upon closer inspection, many items are inexpensive knock-offs. Let the buyer beware! At a voluminous fabric store I purchase several yards in two patterns: blue, tan, and cream feathers; and a geometric teal, beige and black. I'll be sewing new tunics next week.

No visit ashore is complete without a local meal, and the Iguana Cafe's umbrella-covered seating is the perfect place to escape the afternoon heat. The skies clear, the wind dies down, the dust settles, and my drink arrives. Caribbean islands promise leisure a hundred-fold, and Curaçao does not disappoint.

Daily Position: N 12º 07' 02", W 068º 56' 04"
Status: In Port, Willemstad, Curaçao
Weather: Few clouds, 29º C, SE 17 kts, 1 m swell

Daily Position: N 11º 16' 24" W 075º 25' 36"
Status: Underway, Western Caribbean Sea
Weather: partly cloudy, 31º C, E 19 kts, 1 m waves

Down here in the western Caribbean things proceed at a slower pace. It is the Mediterranean without the pretension. The countries here are poor and they know it. Jungle is everywhere, and where there is no jungle there is swamp. Jungle and swamp come right down to the shore. Into a slow, moist, and steamy August we continue a lazy transit toward the entrance of the Panama Canal, skirting lush green islands and guano-capped rocks, heading west and then southwest towards the northeastern coast of Panama.

Ed and I spend the day's idle hours making a poster to show friends and family watching tomorrow's canal transit live via internet. The poster features a colorful compass rose, and we will hold it proudly aloft. Our work will join signs made by other passengers, some with humorous slogans like "sorry kids, spent it all!" and "get me off this ship!"

Getting to the Pacific became an obsession for explorers after Columbus returned with native stories of a "vast open ocean" to the west, across a narrow strip of land. Columbus spent much of his fourth expedition looking for a sail-able inlet. Balboa crossed the isthmus overland in 1513, 500 years ago, to "discover" the South Sea, renamed *Mar Pacifico* less than 10 years later by Ferdinand Magellan. Four hundred more years were to pass, with the low but formidable Continental Divide stubbornly blocking a more direct passage to the Pacific. In all that time, rounding Cape Horn was the fastest sea route to the west, a route that would claim hundreds of ships and thousands of lives. A mid-19th century railroad saw heavy use ferrying gold prospectors to and from California. To mark its 100th birthday, the original canal will soon welcome a second, larger sibling.

We approach the coast in the early dark, prowling the very track Columbus must have taken. The ship is alive with excitement. The lights on shore sparkle, the canal clearly visible from our anchorage. Away to port, a monkey howls, safe from us in the lonely jungle.

It is thrifty to prepare today for the wants of tomorrow.
~ *Aesop*

> *Confidence is the key to all the locks.*
> *~ Joe Paterno*

10

The anticipation which has dominated the last few days has given way to a fine morning, overcast but still clear and bright. Gazing southeast from our anchorage across a mirror-like sea, the port of Colon at the northwestern terminus of the Panama Canal is before me. Mist rises from the golden surface, promising a tropical steam bath on an already hot day. A flock of pelicans flies below in perfect V-formation. Their wing tips gently tease ripples from the surface as if taunting the placid water, looking for fish. Aside the muted morning sounds of a working ship in the tropics, it is purely quiet and serene.

But this is not to last. A small black and white boat gives a merry toot to announce the canal pilot. She embarks by accommodation ladder on the starboard side and moves purposefully to the bridge. Her job is to direct the crew during every minute of today's eight-hour transit to the Pacific. It is disappointing not to stop for a visit in Cristobal or Balboa, to walk The Bridge of The Americas, or to sample empanadas, yuca frita, or sancocho stew. A canal transit is all business.

Placed in service in 1914, I arrive during the canal's 100th operational year. We are one of almost a million ships to transit in that time. As an engineering achievement, the canal is often considered one of the Seven Wonders of the modern world. High elevation runoff feeds the central Gatún Lake. That runoff is emptied in both directions through three sets of locks, first raising us through Gatún, then lowering again through Pedro Miguel and Milaflores.

Large, late afternoon thunderdrops spatter the deck, a brilliant white sun sinking in the west. I am only 30 days from completing this voyage. Western North America, Hawaii, and the islands of the South Pacific promise more adventure. Reflecting on shortcuts and passages and time, and in an ozone-charged breeze, I breathe deep and find myself thinking of home.

Daily Position: N 9º 04' 48", W 079º 40' 48"
Status: North to south transit through Panama Canal Locks
Weather: mostly cloudy, 28º C, light airs, locks calm

Daily Position: N 7º 31' 02" W 082º 37' 48"
Status: southwesterly then northwesterly courses
Weather: high scattered clouds, 28º C, SW 9 kts, 1 m swell

Lost in the mists of morning, the low verdant islands of western Panama appear suddenly from the fog, ahead and well to starboard. The Pacific upholds its namesake quality today, and welcomes my arrival with openly blue skies and lazy, puffy clouds. The course is westerly, to round Isla de Cobia and turn northward by the afternoon. The swells are long and rolling and smooth, not choppy and quick as they were in the Atlantic. The water is so much more blue, a big ocean blue even this close to shore. The water is no longer an accessory to the land. Water here is unbound and free to be water again.

Coffee is the order of the morning and like a zombie I join the throng flocking to the pot. It's the same daily grind though, not anything fresh and Central American. Bummer. On board you get what you get. I grab a bottle of chocolate syrup to make a "mess deck mocha." It is a change from the ordinary and soon everyone at my breakfast club table is mixing in the syrup. We all collude on the daily riddle and are first to catch the ship's representative with our answer: four ducks. The answer is right! More low-quality champagne for us. Oh joy.

Energy restored by the caffeine and chocolate, it is time to walk the decks. A brown booby flock drifts landward on the port side. Seeing the tropical birds in flight snaps me back to where I am, and I remember my pre-sailing regimen of vaccinations. Here in the tropics lurk terrible diseases such as malaria, yellow fever, typhoid, and strains of hepatitis - all diseases from which I am now (hopefully) immune. Thankfully, well to sea, disease-carrying mosquitoes are few.

The day passes like recent others, helping frantic passengers with technology and singing with the passenger choir. Others join a top-side party after supper, but I spend a quiet hour at the rail, watching a radiant sunset give way to a blinding lightning storm. Under electric skies, a brisk breeze knots my hair and the warm rain finally comes.

Fair winds and following seas from one sailor to another!
(Backer John W. Pruitt, III)

> *What would life be if we had no courage to attempt anything?*
> *~ Vincent Van Gogh*

5

Long rolling swells took me right to sleep last night, but at 4:00 a.m. the scream of hydraulic davits jangles me awake. We embark our local pilot to assist the final approach through the Gulf of Nicoya toward Puntarenas. Swells still fetch up from the southwest and break gently on the crunchy tan crystals of granite that form a driftwood-strewn beach.

Another month has passed without a buyer for our house. Ed makes a payment directly from savings, money that would have otherwise been used for activities on this trip. We must start scaling back. But today, I insist on taking a zip line adventure through the jungle.

Nowhere in all the world have I seen such a concentration of wildlife as under the leafy canopy of Costa Rica. Minutes from the ship, a family of howler monkeys swings by, with shimmering obsidian coats and shiny black eyes as big as grapes. They hang by their feet to watch me pass. Fuzzy yellow tussock moth larvae, dark groove-billed ani, leafcutter ants all in line, a dozen greasy crocodiles sunning on a sloppy clay bank, and trilling parrots in a feathered rainbow of hues. It is their domain and they know I am here, but all watch dolefully and without fear. "Just another tourist," the locals seem to say.

I put on climbing gear and complete a mandatory safety brief. Getting up and through the zip line course is sweaty work, but the large banana and coconut leaves keep me cool, and zipping at high speed down the double line helps too. The exhilaration I feel, and yes, the fatigue, underscores the wisdom of doing this world-circling adventure while I still can, before whatever next unknown strikes me down - or even worse, sneaks slowly upon me.

The locals are wrapping up a holiday weekend and vendors are out in force. For $2, the coconut man opens me a fresh nut and hands it over with a straw. Bare footprints in the sand mark my steps as I happily sip, then a distant whistle blows and it's time to sail away.

> **Daily Position:** N 9º 58' 01", W 084º 50' 03"
> **Status:** In Port, Puntarenas, Costa Rica for the rainforest
> **Weather:** mostly cloudy, 29º C, S 10 kts, 1 m chop

Daily Position: N 11º 56' 02" W 090º 29' 24"
Status: At Sea, El Salvador to starboard
Weather: partly cloudy, 32º C, E 12 kts, 1 m swell

Back underway, the start of five days at sea. We navigate west-northwest, with Central America on our starboard side. The sky remains unsettled as I step on deck in the relative coolness of morning. Back at the fantail our propellers keep on churning, generating a roiling wake filled with bubble and spray. Those stalwart propellers have carried us this far, with no real complaints. Like faithful friends, they ask for nothing, are always there, and help turn dreams into memories. Without those propellers this dream would have been over before it began. I settle into a deck chair with a book and read all morning, until the heat of the day forces me back inboard.

Under my cabin door, I discover an itemized bill for last month's shipboard expenses. It is interesting to see in black and white just how those little daily decisions can add up over time. Ed recalls the monthly chow bill during his lengthy deployments. Back then he paid by check, which took the ship months to cash. Nowadays the charge is already on my credit card. An unexpected bonus this month is the exchange rate. The ship makes all charges using Australian currency, and the exchange with U. S. Dollars gives me a 10% discount. I appreciate the bonus, because the exchange rate was reversed when I started.

Ed tells me his watch is broken, but also that he was the first to report the right answer to the daily riddle, scoring us more champagne for the dinner table. While I was relaxing topside he was updating our online photo journal and organizing images. The collection is now over 15,000 shots and 200 gigabytes and should keep him busy for a while.

So here I am, back to underway routine, with choir practice, laundry, and the lively evening meal, sharing stories with my tablemates. Piano virtuoso Mickey Finn and his wife Cathy Reilly (a former Miss Delaware) came aboard in Panama, and they put on an excellent show for the other passengers. Before I know it the evening trivia game is over and it is time to "hit the rack."

You can't start the next chapter of your life if you keep re-reading the last one. ~ Michael McMillan

> All journeys have secret destinations of which the traveler is unaware.
> ~ Martin Buber

5

Early in the morning I am jostled awake by waves pounding on the hull. First the sound of a low "boom" from near the bow, then the shivering vibration down the length of the hull, then a sinister "fizzzz!" of salt spray against the outboard porthole of my cabin.

We are navigating adjacent Acapulco, Mexico, where the warm counter-equatorial current meets the cold California current, and the tranquil weather of the tropics is undeniably behind us. Lightning flashes all around in a pre-breakfast storm that draws both passengers and crew up on deck. We are all prepared for the weather, clad in full rain suits, but we wisely stand well back from the rail. One wrong slip on the turbulent twisting deck could mean a dangerous swim. The ocean is angry. The elemental power of wind and water is all around us, irrepressible, relentless, and invigorating.

Since I'm already up, I dress for the day and spend time updating my journal. Ed locates his backup watch, the one showing three time zones: the time here, the time at home, and Greenwich Mean Time. **Z**ero hour comes for the daily riddle contest, but the prize has already been claimed. I eat a late breakfast and make it to choir practice early. It is the final rehearsal before tomorrow's performance and the music sounds quite polished. In the afternoon the galley crew surprises us with a chocolate demo (and samples). I help teach another juggling class, this time behind the wheelhouse to avoid the rain. It is a good class with over a dozen fellow passengers, and it is nice to see good progress by all the returning students.

Tonight we have plans to meet our Sydney friends for dinner up on deck. The meal starts with artichoke spinach dip, then filet mignon for Ed and tuna steak for me. Halfway through the meal, the rain starts and we drag our table under cover. Everything at sea, even a special dinner, conforms to the whims of the weather.

Daily Position: N 15º 32' 42", W 098º 07' 04"
Status: west-northwesterly course, Mexico to starboard
Weather: dark & cloudy, 29º C, SE 23 kts, 1 m swell

Daily Position: N 19º 17' 48" W 105º 25' 01"
Status: Underway, Pacific Ocean making 21 kts
Weather: scattered clouds, 29º C, W 11 kts, 2 m swell

Noises that once kept me on edge have faded into the background. Like the roar of traffic by a highway or sirens in the city, I no longer hear the constant hiss of ventilation, the rumble of the engines down below, or the crew going about their business in the passageways at night. Changes to the pattern are obvious. A door slams on the cabin next door. The new people are not like the old people. The new people come and go with a bang - literally. They play music late into the night. Even their speech is loud. I know of their relationship troubles, the names of their children, what color nail polish the lady wears, and more, in detail. They will leave the ship in Los Angeles. I have never met these people. I hope to never meet these people.

Gathering with my regular crowd for breakfast, Larraine tells of one "new chum" berating a member of the ship's crew after missing the daily riddle contest - their answer was correct, but it came in too late. We all have a good laugh, because we know the prize is really not worth so much trouble. People can get too worked up indulging an overblown competitive streak. Then Larraine springs the rest of the story: she herself was first to report the correct answer! Yet another bottle of cheap champagne for us. We intend to keep winning until the bottles are gone.

Afternoon arrives. Mexico is still to starboard as we continue our sea passage toward California. Ed does laundry. We both attend the pop choir rehearsal at 12:30 p.m. The music sounds good and the concert at 2:00 p.m. draws a fine crowd. We really nail the performance, and get a standing ovation. For non-musician me, it is a big deal.

At dinner, my tablemates Karen and Roger are feeling under the weather. They excuse themselves early. The rest of us finish the champagne. The galley must have heard about this morning's shouting match, because they put out not one but *two* scrumptious chocolate desserts. Nothing like a little chocolate to calm everyone down, right? Definitely works for me.

The foolish man seeks happiness in the distance;
the wise man grows it under his feet. ~ James Oppenheim

> *It is a true gift to have the opportunity to travel*
> *this miracle of a planet. (Backer James Young)*

7

DAY 81 · NORTH PACIFIC OCEAN · AUGUST 8

Getting back into the groove is always hard. After each of my brain surgeries it took a year to really feel like myself again. The days before each procedure were a lot like getting ready for an extended trip. Pack your bags, clean the house, pay the bills, get papers in order. The big day arrives and you put the past behind. Then wake up to a new day, a new circumstance, and the great unpredictable future. The old comfortable patterns are gone. New routines during travel are like new routines after surgery. But new routines are not all bad. You have passed through the open door, have stepped forward into the great unknown. The "getting ready" anxiety is finally gone. Soon the new patterns become regular patterns, and are finally comfortable old patterns again. I am comfortable here, settled into my traveling home, floating slowly around a watery blue planet. It took this long to find comfort again.

We are to the west of the Baja Peninsula, heading north-northwest, and will continue on similar headings until shortly before arrival at Los Angeles. Atmospheric pressure is on the rise again and Ed has a headache. I do laundry. At lunch I meet a juggler who came aboard in Costa Rica. He plans to stage a show for the passengers tomorrow.

Keeping with recent tradition, my friends and I fan out across the ship, but we are too late with our daily riddle answer. The crew solicits passenger photos for a contest; Ed submits his picture of the lightning from Tuesday. Our collection of photos has grown and grown. A lifetime of memories.

The evening is upon me. The ship hosts a formal night to bid farewell to passengers leaving us on Saturday. I wear my new outfit from India, a delicate print on cotton with turquoise embroidery and matching shawl. My regular companions are all here tonight, and we crack a reserve bottle of prize champagne. Smartly dressed, we again toast ourselves with irreverent formality.

Daily Position: N 23º 49' 36", W 112º 10' 17"
Status: Underway, west of Mexico
Weather: high cumulus, 25º C, NW 9 kts, light chop

Daily Position: N 29º 38' 24" W 116º 25' 18"
Status: Pacific Ocean making 21 kts
Weather: overcast, 12º C, NW 35 kts, 8 m waves

Last-minute activity fills the hours. Los Angeles is the homeport of our ship's parent company. Many of the staff will rotate ashore for time off. A senior steward, Donnie, remarks about the possible delays getting ashore. He expects a repeat of the security delays we experienced in New York. Scrutiny was especially harsh for certain nationalities. He is Filipino and takes the extra checks as a personal affront. A port call with time ashore is a chance to call home, restock supplies, send off some mail. With all this on the line, of course he and his countrymen would not cause trouble.

As the rest of us scramble to get ready for port, the bridge team keeps a steady north-northwest track parallel to the coast of Mexico, the Baja Peninsula well clear to starboard. I think back to my second craniotomy during the year I lived in San Diego. We will pass there in the night.

Two weeks at sea since New York. The short-timers, sailing only for the east-to-west passage, have been cutting corners on laundry. The smell makes it obvious. Days in the sweaty tropics have not helped, either. The aroma of poorly-washed garb wafts through the corridors. "If I can make it just one more day, I will be ashore," they must be telling themselves. Those of us living aboard for the long voyage are not fooled. We can tell they are washing clothes in the cabin sink. Certainly the fight for open machines is a bother, but stinkiness might be a flogging offense in close quarters, such as when packed in a lift.

The Northern Hemisphere is heading into autumn, and on my morning walk I feel the cold. I am at breakfast by 9:00 a.m. The galley team hosts a culinary demonstration. I prep, then teach another technology class. The satellite internet connection slows to a trickle: fairly standard on the day before a port call as follow-on arrangements get made. I have plans to see family, and they are expecting me.

To end the day, Ed makes another "volcano" sundae disappear, living up to his nickname, Eddie Ice Cream.

10

It's wonderful to travel with somebody you love and we never travel anywhere without one another. ~ Roger Moore. (Backers Nancy & Jack Almeida)

Sailing

Segment

Five

> *It's kind of fun to do the impossible.*
> *~ Walt Disney*

2♦

ranes line the wharf, indistinct sil-houettes of bare steel against the sickly orange hills, like oil der-ricks in the desert. Instead of sucking up black gold with a rhythmic up and down, they move side-to-side, pluck-ing valuable cargo that was floated here from a hundred exotic ports. The crane operators deftly swap inbound finished goods - toys, electronics, and clothing - for raw materials from North America. The freighters will be loaded by afternoon and then head back to sea, plying the ship-ping lanes on an inexorable quest to trade proximity for profit.

The local pilot comes aboard at 4:15 a.m. to guide us northbound through the buoyed channel into San Pedro. The wind is calm, the marine layer lingers, and smog obscures the skyline. Disembarking passengers scramble down the brow, frazzled and scowling, in compe-tition with the bustling and efficient ship's crew. Friends mention plans to visit Universal Studios, Hollywood Boulevard, and the Chinese Theatre's famous collection of concrete hand and footprints.

I am scheduled for a telephone interview with DJ Grandpa, a fol-low-up for his weekly broadcast about inspirational Kickstarter proj-ects. My cell phone is back on the network with five bars. Being con-nected feels tangibly strange, almost uncomfortable, like wearing shoes on the wrong feet. I find I haven't missed the telephone at all.

elatives from both sides of my family live in southern California. Uncle Charlie picks me up to join Aunt Jane and several of my cousins (plus their children!) at their home. It is a happy gather-ing with food, laughter, and storytelling, and then the surprise: cake and ice cream in celebration of Ed's birthday, which is tomorrow. My soul is recharged and ready to tackle the last three weeks at sea.

Outside the breakwater and with Catalina Island to starboard, we enter the traffic sepa-ration scheme and begin the long westbound ocean passage to the Big Island of Hawaii.

Daily Position: N 33º 43' 45", W 118º 15' 43"
Status: In Port, Los Angeles, USA
Weather: Sunny & clear, 19º C, SE 6 kts, harbor calm

Across the Pacific we go, on a great circle route to paradise. It is Ed's birthday, a birthday at sea. In the last three months, we have made good friends among the crew. They surprise him with a bunch of balloons, a signed card, and poster on our cabin door. He carries the card and a pen the rest of the day, collecting additional signatures. Much more than a souvenir or a photograph, a collection of signatures is a sharply personal way to mark a point in time. With a few strokes of ink, each person leaves a part of themselves on the page. This exact collection of people will disperse and never be together again. But we will remember when they *were* here with us, with each signature as proof. And the miles continue to slip by like days in a lifetime, soft and steady beneath the keel.

Sunday routine is posted and Sunday cooking smells waft lazily from the galley. Brunch is a comfortable weekly event. Sunday routine means time to catch up on sleep, write letters, press and fold laundry, and organize anything overlooked during the week. This down day is well timed after a frantic port call, and the common areas are uncharacteristically quiet. Some longtime passengers (who have been aboard since Sydney) disembarked yesterday to tour more of the States. With a start, I realize why the place seems empty. Familiar faces are gone from their familiar places. I will never see those smiling faces again.

As with other sailing segments, new passengers are with us. This batch seems better behaved. I discover most are Aussies catching a ride home. A group of Hawaiians is heading home too, eager to spread the Aloha Spirit. They advertise ukulele lessons, and later in the day hold a class in the ancient art of hula. I jump in to learn the moves. The music takes me right back to countless hours I spent as a child, learning dance routines and practicing body isolations.

Night falls, the bridge retards ship's clocks to match the next time zone, and we all get an extra hour of blissful sleep.

Birthdays are good for your health.
The more you have, the longer you live.

106

> *The sky seemed to clear, then I realized it was not a rift in the clouds but the white crest of an enormous wave. ~ Ernest Shackleton*

Under a dense blanket of lingering cloud, a long and rolling northeast swell catches the ship on the starboard quarter, a forceful and regular shove. I feel our westward movement in every step of my gait, transmitted to my feet by the surging deck. My sea legs are steady and I move with the practiced grace of an old salt, skipping lightly above the teak on the sticky tips of rubber soles. But something seems different.

On the beam a dull gray sea of tiny ripples stretches to the horizon, where all that gray turns abruptly into a single uncontested triumphant line of blue, a heroic blue, a terrible blue, a taut blue cord dividing ocean and sky, like the sharp edge of wide eyes in the moonlight. It beckons from the horizon at all quarters and then it comes closer, first grasping, then pulsing, reaching down across the waves, breathing out until the entire surface brims blue, dark and sinister, gobbling up the gray and leaving the lower world in stark contrast to the sky above. The sky is crisp, a springtime sky, dry and crackling, aglow with a blindingly complete and unblemished light, a perfect blue too glorious to grasp. Washed to the east by this relentless blue, the clouds have gone.

It is a typical day underway: an ample breakfast with heaps of fresh melon (while it lasts), choir, hula class, reading in canvas chairs on deck. The galley serves lunch a tad late, but no one really minds - it is a "pub lunch" and it sticks to my ribs. Formal for dinner, right on schedule. I wear a green velvet dress and pearls. Ever the gossip, Larraine dishes a juicy rumor: a new chum has washed laundry in the hot tub. Full points for creativity, mate, but the inevitable explosion of suds means the tub's lengthy closure.

After dinner the dark blue line is back, taunting me, teasing its way across the horizon under pinkening, bushy clouds. Elegant in my finery and with a big smile, I shield my eyes from the brilliant light of the setting sun and fix the sparkling blue forever in my mind.

Daily Position: N 29º 22' 12'', W 133º 11' 54''
Status: Underway, Pacific Ocean making 20 kts
Weather: Sunny & dry, 23º C, NW 5 kts, 1 m swells

Daily Position: N 26º 13' 48" W 141º 40' 13"
Status: Underway, Pacific Ocean making turns for 22 knots
Weather: Sunny, 25º C, SE 15 kts, 2 m rollers

Keeping to the proper track in the open ocean is an ongoing act of love. The rudder may hold straight, but the currents move to and fro beneath us. A strange swell sets up a rolling motion that moves the stern through a drifting corkscrew one minute, a figure eight the next. The conning officer is like a wrangler with a cane switch, nudging a reluctant elephant back in line.

"Nothing travels faster than a rumor aboard ship" is the old adage. Yesterday's drama at the pool must be true: new rules circulate. "The Captain is fed up with ship's laundry complaints, and has directed the purser to sell tickets for the laundry queue." This is the buzz at least, and over coffee my friends and I share a hearty chuckle at the notion. I have already done wash today, and know the rumor is totally untrue. Is this just playful ribbing by full timers (like us) at the expense of the new hands? So many rumors: "Since we sailed, five people have died." "The engineer uses this cheap champagne to degrease his machinery." "The cook has run out of American-style bacon." How do they start? Which are based in truth? They come and go like sea birds on the wind.

Still, life at sea goes on. I spend time cleaning up my cabin. Straightening is a welcome and uncomplicated task after considering all those crazy rumors. I gather similar items together and start sizing up luggage space for the pack out. I have kept souvenirs to a minimum, but there is no way all this stuff will ever fit back into my suitcases.

The corkscrew roll has me feeling off, so I drink lots of tea and focus on routine: a good choir rehearsal, hula class, journal, reading and a nap. At the evening meal I try to stay healthy with a fruit entrée and light flaky fish for the main.

Topside the sky is pink, and wispy clouds mark our return to warmer weather. Tomorrow we will cross the Tropic of Cancer for the fourth and last time on our westward journey around the world. Showers of meteors, the annual Perseids, light the sky above.

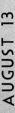

Seek not to become extraordinary in an ordinary realm,
but rather to become ordinary in an extraordinary realm.

> *Do just once what others say you cannot do, and you will never pay attention to their limitations again.* ~ James Cook

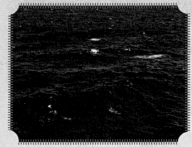

Grudgingly still awake at 2:00 a.m., I see Ed at his computer. He is catching a satellite signal to pay our bills. The house still hasn't sold and he remarks that money is tight. This crazy corkscrew motion jostles me in the rack. I toss and turn for hours, then wake with a start. I have almost missed breakfast: fresh fruit, salmon with capers, and tomato juice with lemon. I step topside to curse the cause of my insomnia. Choppy whitecaps top the crests of loping swells. A sturdy wind drives us before it. We are caught in the flow, a plunging seesaw of pitch.

The strong east wind comes with another surprise. The wind is from directly astern, and blows at the exact same speed as the ship. This means the engine exhaust, cigarette smoke, and other smells emitted by the engineers (I invite your imagination) stagnate around us and linger. We could change course to either side of the wind line and escape, but the bridge team presses onward and the yellow cloud surrounding us blooms larger with each passing hour.

By afternoon my weekly passel of laundry is folded and stowed away. Ed is learning ukulele from the Hawaiian passengers and plays me "Jumping Flea." He is victim to "string teacher's revenge" - sore fingertips. Choir practice goes well but is lightly attended. Many singers are preparing for the passenger talent show, which opens to a packed house. The crew especially enjoys seeing our varied talents on display.

Mark Twain spent four months in Hawaii in 1866, and in his lectures called the place "the loveliest fleet of islands that lies anchored in any ocean." He returned in 1895 with a fervent desire to get ashore, but saw his "dream of 29 years go to ruin": a cholera epidemic in Honolulu trapped him at anchor less than a mile away. He continued on around the world, but no subsequent adventure would ever dull his longing for the islands. Ed and I will make our own return visit in the morning, and there is no epidemic to stop us.

Daily Position: N 22º 37' 54", W 149º 37' 46"
Status: Underway as before, Pacific Ocean
Weather: partly cloudy, 28º C, E 18 kts, 2 m swells

Daily Position: N 19º 49' 23" W 155º 05' 37"
Status: In port, Hilo, Big Island of Hawaii, USA
Weather: partly cloudy, 29º C, NE 5 kts, 1 m waves

DAY 88

HILO, HAWAII

AUGUST 15

For today's adventure I will help new friends Roger and Karen return souvenirs and extra luggage to their home in Kona. The town is on the other side of the island, however, and timing will be tight. We embark the local pilot at 8:00 a.m. and proceed into Hilo Harbor. It is good to see a Coast Guard buoy tender hard at work setting aids to navigation. "The bridge of a cutter is the best office in the world, after a helicopter cockpit of course," says Ed.

Offloaded and rolling, I drive along the Big Island's north coast and stop to walk beneath lush vegetation and over jagged lava ("a'a") along the shore. The locals say, "if you plant a pink eraser, it will grow you a pencil." Flowers consume the view in all directions, the xylem flowing and alive with jungle magic, wide petals of pink, salmon, crimson, and mustard, blooming perfectly and without intervention. Paradise is all around and unavoidable. An wave of awareness hits me: beauty is not limited to just here, halfway around the globe. Beauty is worth taking time. You cannot wait for an invitation. You must go and *seek it out*.

At the Waipio Lookout my gaze drifts from the horizon's angry sea into a ravine, an inlet that was wiped out by a tsunami several decades ago. In Honoka'a town, we stop for lunch - world famous malasadas at the Tex Drive-In. Here the Portuguese fried dough is raised to a high art. You can order traditional buns sprinkled with sugar, or something more fancy and filled with chocolate, whipped cream, or local preserves - a treat well worth the journey from, well, anywhere.

By lunch I am on the western shore, north of Kona, traveling south between jumbled ridges of jagged lava rock, dark as midnight. White rounded stones offset the road, arranged into words and pictograms, stark marks on the vegetation-free terrain. The clock ticks down, and with the sun behind me I race across the saddle between snow-capped Mauna Loa and Mauna Kea to the port, and cross the brow just in time for sailing.

This is the most magnificent, balmy atmosphere in the world, and ought to take dead men out of the grave. ~ Mark Twain

Safe travels on this and all your future "journeys!"
(Backer Charlie Coiro)

6

We pass Maui, Kaho'olawe, Lanai, and Moloka'i in the night and navigate the narrow harbor entrance. We turn and moor port-side-to our berth at Aloha Tower. The cloudless sky promises a fine warm day with very little rain. Of course, this means no rainbows.

I stroll past the image of a young Kahuna in full regalia. He looms three stories tall, his mural a pleasing contrast to slapdash graffiti. In park-like pockets of green the noise of Honolulu traffic fades and quiet settles in. I find one such oasis under the banyan trees on the grounds of 'Iolani Palace, a sacred spot surrounded by sacred stones. The wind catches the wide banyan leaves and berries rain down around me. I escape from under and gambol across a sun-drenched lawn of wide-bladed grass. Rare pink hibiscus flowers flutter in the breeze and fill the air with perfume, sweetly masking the urban odors of trash day.

For lunch I make a beeline to Auntie Pasto's and arrive when they open. This place is one of those rare gems, well off the beaten tourist track and oh so good! I order the daily special: sautéed mushrooms and onions over penne, with roasted garlic and olive oil. A steady stream of locals cycle through and the staff provides attentive but unimposing service. My body warms as the pasta digests. The air conditioning is broken - if it ever worked - but chipped brown ceiling fans whir at full speed, drowning out many wine-fueled conversations.

At a fabric store I buy ten yards of patterned cloth, chosen from multi-hued options on thousands of rolls. Travelex behind the Ala Moana mall helps me swap my entire collection of world currencies for dollars. There is just enough time to make a phone call home. Then darkness settles, Friday night fireworks light the sky above Diamond Head, and to the east a waxing gibbous moon climbs out of our wake. Swaying palms, smoky torches, and soft hula music all fade astern as mighty Oahu sinks into the sea.

Daily Position: N 21º 20' 00", W 157º 50' 00"
Status: In Port, Honolulu, Oahu, Hawaii, USA
Weather: Sunny, 27º C, E 10 kts, 1 m waves

DAY 90

NAWILIWILI, HAWAII

AUGUST 17

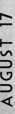

Nawiliwili whispers rural in the way Honolulu screams big city. The island displays her older features well; red-rusted hills shrouded in flowing capes of green. I am off to see Waimea Canyon, the Grand Canyon of the Pacific. The western volcano wall collapsed 4 million years ago, and rainfall on Mount Wai'ale'ale has since eroded the incision, 15 kilometers long and a thousand meters deep. I pause at the summit and look down. Other visitors to the canyon engage in friendly chitchat as we wave to helicopters below the rim. The conversation turns to my illness, and they ask if I have big plans. I say this trip around the world is my version of running a marathon. In the final stretch now, I feel my energy starting to dip.

Chickens are everywhere. Hurricane Iniki destroyed the robust chicken farming operations here in 1992. The long coops are gone but many of the birds escaped, and their wild descendants continue to plague the locals. They joke that the Hawaiian state bird is the chicken. KFC has been redefined Kauai Flattened Chicken, and the phrase is invoked often when out for a drive. Signs admonish everyone not to feed feral chickens. Just a few generations of free competition has adorned the birds with plumage that rivals any long-native tropical species.

Macro and micro culture are also in competition here. The worldwide culture that includes Wal-Mart and Starbucks follows the tourist money. Local culture fights back, at roadside stands that display Ni'ihau shell leis and copra, and serve locally grown and roasted coffee. A sign proclaims *A'ole o Kauai'i 'i o 'Amelika, ā 'a'ole loa e lilo ana* - Kauai'i is not America, and it never will be. Vandals have scraped off the word 'not.'

At the famous spouting horn blowhole, I am showered by spray squeezed aloft by the southern swell. Returning to the ship, I find sailing is delayed while we wait for port clearance. Something is afoot, but mere passengers are never consulted about such things. The culture of those in charge is what matters.

*I have seen so many extraordinary things,
nothing seems extraordinary anymore. ~ Lewis Carroll*

9

oming off of three exciting days ashore, I enjoy sleeping in. Adjusting back to the underway routine is smooth this time, smoother than it has ever been before. First and most important this morning is coffee with the breakfast club. The ship announces a stop to the daily riddle contest. A few zealous competitors set off a volcano of complaints - from others, apparently - certainly not us. With unexpected idle time I help new friend Rick with his tablet, then swing by the cabin before breakfast: pineapple, toast with honey, and orange juice. At trivia with the regulars, my team loses graciously to escape more cheap champagne.

The competitive drama surfaces again at choir practice. Some singers almost come to blows over notes; creative differences, perhaps. We are given a stern talking-to by the directors, and the scolding works. Renewed focus on shared goals yields musical magic. Will it last?

es, regular routine is back and boredom stalks the fringes of the day. An impromptu ragtime concert on piano is a welcome diversion after lunch. Tim Barton is one of the few others aboard from the USA and plays like a dream. I pull a canvas deck chair to the rail and catch up my journaling. The slow rolling waves turn my writing time into nap time, and soon it is time for the evening meal. My regular Aussie tablemates have other plans tonight and so it is just us Yanks. The whole ship seems subdued and regular evening diversions fall flat, so I head back to the cabin and watch a movie on my laptop.

"Beginner's mind" lets you see a place as if for the first time, as a child might. Children wake up to fresh wonder each day. On a short vacation, beginner's mind is easy to find, but extended travel nibbles at the edges of boredom, and I fear the last two weeks of this journey may mask my sense of adventure behind bland repetition. Hoping there is a way to recapture a wide-eyed wonder in the face of the familiar and safe, I drift off to sleep.

Daily Position: N 17º 04' 42", W 160º 54' 12"
Status: Underway, SSW course toward American Samoa
Weather: Sunny, 29º C, E 33 kts, 3 m swells

DAY 91   NORTH PACIFIC OCEAN   AUGUST 18

113

Daily Position: N 10º 17' 02" W 163º 00' 35"
Status: Southerly course 197º, making 21 kts
Weather: Partly cloudy, 28º C, SE 18 kts, 2 m waves

DAY 92

NORTH PACIFIC OCEAN

AUGUST 19

Out on the open ocean once again, steaming south into the tropics. Early clouds drop astern and high pressure is back, pushing the waves smooth like a rolling pin. Swirling tendrils of frothy wash fan out behind us as we skate across the surface at over 20 knots.

Another passenger, Grahme, is making the full circumnavigation after a life-changing injury. He lost his foot and part of his leg in a motorcycle accident. He has since gained fame as a professional sailor, and gives a talk about his experiences entitled "Put Your Best Foot Forward." I stay late to thank him for his inspiring words.

Then I race to grab lunch, but am waylaid by a guy asking about his smartphone. The chow line closes and I have missed the meal! Smartphone guy is long gone, and would not shed a tear for my grumbling tummy. I grab an emergency snack from the cabin and retreat to a reliably private spot: the laundry. Wonderful idea, until passenger Jeff walks in and pleads, "will you help me with my tablet?" It is Groundhog Day with this annoyance of my own making, but he rewards my help with a rumor and a quote. The rumor: someone did their laundry in the hot tub again. We agree the person should be charged for draining, cleaning, filter replacement, and refill. And his quote: "Because of people like that, I will probably never sail again."

World travel is hard, and like anything worth doing, you must tease the tangible benefits from a background of inconvenience, discomfort, and the antics of annoying people. Today the annoyances pile up to overwhelm me. I am "peopled out." Three months trapped at sea with a ship full of strangers will do that.

Dinner brings a dose of "my people" and that really helps; familiar friendly faces and laughter. Maxine and Bruce bring down a quality bottle of Italian wine for us to share. Evening drops a pastel shroud across the sky, salmon pink and powder puff blue competing unsuccessfully with velvety black.

Semper Paratus - Ad Astra
(Backers Scott & Marion Gesele - CGA '92)

> What can we gain by sailing to the moon if we are not able to cross the abyss that separates us from ourselves? ~ Thomas Merton

Smooth and flat, these tropical waters continue to baby the ship. We make over 400 nautical miles on a day that passes quickly, a smooth progression through familiar events: breakfast and coffee, choir practice, laundry, classes, journaling, supper, and after-work amusements. Yesterday's anxiousness - cabin fever, really - has passed. With nowhere to go but onward, I feel the calm acceptance of my benign fate.

Among the crew, the great liberty controversy continues. I am told company regulations require one day on land for every five days at sea. Even adjusted for the sailing schedule, some have not stepped ashore in more than 15 days, and have been given (in their minds, at least) no satisfactory explanation. The totalitarian "because the captain said so" is certainly not a good answer, as the days when a captain could exercise both high and low justice are long gone. Still, the rules under which we operate were not just invented. They grew over time, centuries in some cases. Is the restriction limited to this ship? As in times of old, we hear nothing from the captain. Instead we plod south and the mystery remains unsolved.

At sunset I venture topside to check our position and the weather. The wind is strong from the east, and catches me full in the face. Squinting, my eyes start to water as the wind pushes teardrops back to my ears. Lady Selene is coming up, the centerpiece of another happy coincidence: a full moon at the Equator. With only a month before the autumnal equinox, she rises from the placid waters on our port beam, exactly to the east, and exactly at sunset. Low clouds block my first glimpse, but are spectacle enough by themselves, with tops touched by pink and bottoms that glow and sparkle, unencumbered by man-made lights and atmospheric pollution. The moon's majestic disk finally climbs skyward into the clear, and paints a narrow pathway of silver from my handrail to the horizon.

Daily Position: N 3º 32' 53'', W 165º 03' 12''
Status: SSW course, midway between Hawaii & Samoa
Weather: Sunny, 30º C, E 20 kts, 3 m rolling swell

Daily Position: S 3º 30' 55" W 167º 11' 01"
Status: Crossed the Equator to enter the Southern Hemisphere
Weather: Sunny, 31º C, E 16 kts, 2 m waves

DAY 94

THE EQUATOR

AUGUST 21

Good morning, all ye Honorable Shellbacks, tightwads, one-wires and sharkbait. Know ye that the ship, having arrived at the gates of the South Pacific to be properly inspected by King Neptune, has been found worthy. His most Royal Majesty has conveyed to the ship's Captain the key to Davey Jones' Locker and has granted us passage into his domain. However, several green and unworthy pollywogs invoke a stern command: complete a structured test for saltiness and undergo a ritualistic cleansing, by which they may atone for their various and sundry transgressions against the royal court, and myriad sins of omission, commission, and intermission. At last Neptune releases the ship and company to proceed with alacrity and all due haste across that most illustrious of invisible and arbitrary lines, the Equator. Welcome to the South Pacific, and may ye venture onward with seaweed in your hair, a siren in your ears, and a seagull on your head!

Without a doubt, this is one of the best days of my life. The ship crosses the Equator at 6:14 a.m. To celebrate, the ship's company participates in a "renewal of vows," a traditional initiation rite for those who have never crossed the Equator. Although this happened once earlier in the trip, I missed the chance to participate. Thankfully the Honorable Shellbacks are merciful and I pass all trials with success. Another win for me: in place of riddles, the ship now asks a daily nautical trivia question, and I am first with the correct answer. "When building a ship, where do they always put the last rivet?" Why, in the last hole, of course! Prize champagne for me and my table.

My victories make me so happy, I do not mind being stopped with technology problems. I do not mind spending half the afternoon washing my goop-sludged clothing, fully trashed during the initiation. I do not even mind missing the topside deck party to welcome everyone back to the Southern Hemisphere. Right here, at the planet's waistband, I am on top of the world.

Do you fear death? Do you fear that dark abyss?
All your deeds laid bare? All your sins punished? ~ Davey Jones

Another sweltering tropical day at sea, but the last before a keenly anticipated stop at Pago Pago. Coffee in the commons, computer work, final choir practice and show, evening chow. Predictable. Comfortable. Relaxed. Normal.

The bridge team holds a detailed lecture about their organization, duties, and equipment, a look behind the scenes at their very important world. The occasion shakes me awake to an important oversight: we passengers have grown to take the crew for granted. I may not have not done them justice in this tale. Equipment must be maintained, food prepared and served. Idle hours must be filled, the track line consulted, and positions taken to maintain safe passage. These activities are part of the everyday background, and because they are mundane I have mentioned them with infrequency. But behind all these things lurk the crewmembers, following in-port or at-sea routine. They drive the narrative and direct the energy. It seems like a tightly scripted show, but of course there is no script. The show has a lackluster title - duty - and they all do it well.

Before any port call after a long sea leg, everyone gets fidgety. Those going ashore pack and scramble and say their goodbyes. Only a handful will leave us tomorrow, but in less than two weeks their story will be mine, so this time I start making notes. Today holds a series of "one last time" events. For the last Cruise Critic meeting (always bring your own beverage) I bring my cidre from France. There is no way to carry it back to the States, so I might as well enjoy it now.

Karen and Roger gift me a picture print: me with some feathered dancers, taken during the stopover in Hawaii. Burt and Larraine, ever the lucky ones, claim the final bingo jackpot, and share a pricey bottle of champagne with the table. Each of us raises a toast to their good fortune, for today, the few remaining days of this adventure, and for the unnumbered days that are yet to come.

Daily Position: S 10º 16' 52", W 169º 14' 14"
Status: Underway, South Pacific, turns for 20 kts
Weather: Partly cloudy, 30º C, E 19 kts, 3 m waves

U nveiled as the first misty rays of morning crest the eastern hills and paint gold upon the bushy slopes, Pago Pago's wide harbor entrance beckons. Early 1900s colonial architecture is mixed with the more traditional rounded *fale* dwellings. Legend says the god Tagaloalagi once settled an argument between carpenters with this decree: future houses must match the curve from heaven to horizon. Residents build shrines to their ancestors in the yard: those with exalted status in the front, others (less reputable) in back.

I approach a happily colorful but dilapidated bus and the owner, Vernon, waves me aboard with a warm "talofa!" He says, "This is Samoa: no air conditioning, no seat belts, no problem!" We pass buildings wiped out by the 2009 earthquake and tsunami, but stop to visit a church left miraculously untouched, the altar set about with blooming flowers and aglow with sunlight sparkling through intricate stained glass.

M y driver Tele (Samoan for 'big') sips from a coconut and tells the legend of the fair maiden Sina who, at the request of her spurned lover the eel, buried his head in the sand upon his death. The head grew into a coconut tree, and thereafter any time Sina drank from a coconut she would have to kiss his face. Another legend tells of an old woman and her granddaughter who, to escape starvation, leapt to their deaths from a Vaitogi island cliff. They were transformed into a shark and a turtle, and may still appear when called by song.

I visit the home of the first locally elected governor, marvel at his walking sticks, and relax with mango and punch while Vernon and Tele serenade on the ukulele. We pass Flowerpot Rocks, transformed from drowned lovers Fatu and Futi, each crowned by an umbrella of green.

Safely back in town I bid goodbye ("tofa") to the magical mystery bus, and dally at a tiny museum showing Samoan art and history. Across the brow as the last lines are taken in - earning the steward's reproach - I am away to sea.

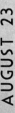

DAY 96

PAGO PAGO, SAMOA

AUGUST 23

The sooner you fall behind the more time you have to catch up. ~ Will Rogers (Backers Angel & JD Henning - CGA 92)

118

> *Tomorrow is a mystical land where 99% of all human productivity, motivation, and achievement is stored.*

5

International travel means an ongoing battle with time zones. Each adjacent zone is separated by an hour, with one exception. At an imaginary line running north and south along the 180th meridian of longitude called the International Date Line, +12 hours and -12 hours meet, and demand a 24-hour time change. Crossing the line easterly, a day would be repeated. But my voyage continues west, so today is both Saturday and Sunday, the two crammed together, an all-at-once payment for the hours we banked through the summer as extra sleep. Three and a half months of progress erased by a rule.

Up early, I shower, then join the impressive coffee queue in the galley. My regular mates shout and gesture at the starboard porthole. The flying fish are all around, flashing silvery fins. Some land, flopping, on deck. Helpful shoes nudge them back over the side. The swell is long and rolling. Short windy breaths add stippled texture to the surface like gentle puffs across prairie grass. Cumulus thunderheads build skyward, stark white and gray. They form mushrooms of moisture, anchored on stalks of water. If we change course early enough, the torrential pillars are avoidable. The bridge team threads the slalom course with ease, and the decks stay dry.

In the afternoon I catch up on my journal and take a spin on the exercise bike. It is one of the last warm days before returning to winter in the Southern Hemisphere. I overhear a bookish lady talking to friends. She claims we only lost a half day crossing the dateline, and cites this morning's mess deck church service on "Saturday" as proof. She then reveals she woke in the middle of the night when we crossed the Equator to see her drain water change direction. She would probably believe me if I urged her to watch for an actual line in the water as we cross the dateline. Sometimes it is better just to listen and leave silly notions unaddressed.

Daily Position: S 16º 49' 30", W 176º 11' 11"
Status: Underway, crossed International Date Line
Weather: Partly cloudy, 27º C, SE 16 kts, 1 m chop

DAY 98

SUVA, FIJI

AUGUST 26

At anchor, silent and rusty, a dozen white tuna boats welcome us. They fly the host country flag at the masthead, and home country flags at the stern: China, Kiribati, the Marshall Islands. In the port, dusty buses in crayon colors bring workers from outer villages. I board a now-empty bus and wish I had worn a sports bra as we bounce out of town. A sign in English proclaims Fiji Bitter to be 'The Taste of Fiji!' Everyone gives a thumbs up and shouts a hearty "Bula!" There are no scowls, only wide smiles and crow's feet.

Towns here band together for mutual benefit, residents often closely related. Each household provides some service to the collective whole. A fenced yard is frowned upon, but there are fences still, often around cleaner houses and newer cars. Dwellings stand on concrete stilts to cool and to avoid burrowing insects. Livestock are tethered where the grass is greenest. A large sow roots in the mud around a huge tree root - she is better than a bulldozer. Slopes are covered with broad leaf crops in low orderly rows of taro, ginger, kava, turmeric, sugar cane, and tobacco.

On the western bank of the Rewa river I board a wooden launch, painted turquoise and propelled by a blackened outboard spewing noxious, oily smoke. From my vantage in the bow, I wave to a clutch of small children playing along the freshly dredged channel, then disembark at the Rewa Secondary School. A sign at the entrance proclaims their intent to "train the soul, train the mind, train the hands." The kids here are poor but don't know it - they are rich in love and learning.

Back upriver I join a town gathered for the traditional kava welcome ceremony. The milky drink is smooth, with a subtle earthy taste - perhaps a bit peppery - and it quickly numbs my lips and tongue. Ed gives a speckled nautilus shell a hearty blast, and the kids pile around to flash playful fingers as their elders drum, sing, and dance up a sweat. Under monochromatic blue skies, I reluctantly return to Suva and the fast-paced modern world.

Twenty years from now you will be more disappointed by the things that you didn't do than by the ones you did do. - Mark Twain

Zone after watery time zone, we have nearly circled the planet. The enormity of the effort over the past three months hits me fully and finally as a wave of amazement, but also sadness. The long days of discovery are at an end. Just two ports and three more days at sea separate me from the goal. My body reacts in the same way it does when I think about dying. THE END. So final. I have so much more I want to do, so much more I want to see, so many things to say to so many people, and there will not be time to do, see, or say any of them. No more time lady - you have used it all. If there is any lesson it is this: use each moment well. I have just a week to get my affairs in order before stepping across the brow one last time, to leave this short shipboard life behind for an uncertain future, swirling hidden in the mists of tomorrow.

No time to waste, but I waste it just the same on one more uninterrupted day of blissful avoidance. A late morning lecture covers our next stops in New Zealand: the port of Auckland and the Bay of Islands. And laundry, endless laundry. Life can be measured in trips to the laundry. Choir separates washing and drying, and my clothes are ready after a solid rehearsal. We perform in formal black and white to a packed house, a program heavy with Australian patriotism that ends with hugs, exchanged addresses, and promises to write.

Following standard routine for two-nights-out, the evening meal is formal. Ed wears his military tuxedo with full medals and I don a navy dress and all my (few pieces of) jewelry. We uncork one of the 'prize winning' bottles of champagne, the one with the silver label. Table 108 finishes the evening packed into seats for the final production show, La Fiesta.

Night falls and it is abruptly cold. We cross the Tropic of Capricorn, to exit the tropics for the last time. Relentless waves build into monsters on the bow, and I shiver as the piercing winds of winter tug the hem of my lacy dress.

Daily Position: S 24º 13' 01", E 177º 00' 48"
Status: Course SSW, South Pacific Ocean
Weather: Mostly cloudy, 20º C, S 21 kts, 2 m swells

DAY 100

SOUTH PACIFIC OCEAN

AUGUST 28

Everything good must come to an end, as sunset follows the dawn. A hard deadline always helps focus my attention, and with a scheduled return to Sydney in just four days, it is time to get serious about the onward journey. The ship obediently continues on a south-south-westerly course while we passengers scramble to organize baggage and pack baubles collected across six continents.

Ed makes an early morning call to Boston - where it is late afternoon yesterday - then swings by the cabin and escorts me to breakfast: an ample brunch with friends in the main galley. We are summoned to a last-minute choir rehearsal. Surprise surprise: no singing but glasses of champagne instead, to celebrate our musical achievements throughout the summer. The choir directors Alan and Alana invite everyone to visit them at their home in England. It is a tearfully happy goodbye.

In the afternoon I head to the laundry to beat the expected last-minute crush. Drama always attends the laundry, and today is no different. The ship's movement sets a dryer door swinging, and I lean on it to avoid injury. A wild-haired shoeless man enters, looks across the room, then realizes his wash is two decks below. A red-eyed woman squeezes in and starts to sneeze, uncontrollably. Thankfully I am done and back out with haste to avoid the expanding cloud of germs. Something about a public laundry always makes me feel like I am back at college.

While packing I consider things I have learned on this journey. When the ship sails, all debts are paid. A Greek fisherman's hat hugs the head in high winds. Do not cross the gangway holding anything important, especially your keys. On travel most objects demand a disposable re-lationship, especially paper: itineraries, receipts, maps. A common currency is a blessing. There is a benefit to going ashore in disguise. Avoid tourists, even if it means more walking. Each experience may seem an insignificant dot in the grand story, but each dot is always indispensable when looking back.

Don't cry because it's over. Smile because it happened.
~ Dr. Seuss

122

> *We weren't lost. We were just exploring.*
> *(Backer Chris Conway)*

8

Hopelessly early in the morning, we navigate south through the well-marked Rangitoto Channel and to our berth at Prince's Wharf. It is chilly and wet, a miserable late winter morning. I follow commuters in galoshes and slickers to a covered ferry crossing the harbor at 21 knots. Regulars flash chip cards to check on and off, but I must pay cash. Cushy bench seats nestle under silver-framed, rain-spattered windows, and life jackets are stored in the overhead. At the far terminal, I order espresso at a tiny shop, 100-year-old coffee pots and bean grinders on display. A Segway tour tempts me, but not in this wind.

Down a brick-lined alley decorated with antiques, I find a hole-in-the-wall cafe and arrange their wrought iron furniture for lunch. The meal is the very definition of trendy: salmon and spinach quiche with a buttery corrugated crust, arugula salad with creamy caper dressing topped by hand-placed carrot and red onion slices, and individual pots of tea sweetened with local honey.

Onward to my only planned destination, the Devonport Chocolate factory on Wynyard Street. A lady in a red raincoat walks her fluffy white poodle past a colorful reminder about Father's Day. The sign recommends a funny chocolate mustache lollipop for dad. In the show room, little confectionery works of art beckon from tray upon chocolatey tray: mint melt, cappuccino, Valencia orange, limoncello. I share a pair of heavenly cherry-topped truffles with my stalwart traveling companion and the crazy love of my life, Edward. In this rare magical moment I can forget about the rain.

Puddles fill the street, so I duck into a used bookshop. Books are frozen snapshots in the torrent of time. They collect in such shops, the loosely related titles swirled together in themed piles of karmic debris. It is exciting to think that my own little story may come here to rest some day. First, I must complete the journey.

Daily Position: S 36º 50' 25'', E 174º 44' 23''
Status: In Port, Auckland, New Zealand
Weather: overcast, showers, 16º C, NW 10 kts, 2 m waves

Daily Position: S 35º 12' 04" E 174º 10' 17"
Status: Riding Port Anchor, Bay of Islands, New Zealand
Weather: Mostly cloudy, 14º C, NW 9 kts, bay calm

The unexpected sudden calmness after rounding the promontory of Cape Brett wakes me early. I roll from the rack, turn my gaze to the porthole, and gasp, for what I see literally takes my breath away. Faceted rocks grow from a golden fog, distinct and darkly sinister, back-lit by a piercing sunrise. We seem to float upon a sepia cloud, as a dozen jagged islands stream past at 20 knots, just out of reach, nautical asteroids shrouded in dangling green and cradled by the mist. A buoy marking Jellicoe Channel shatters the illusion as we anchor abeam Motukokako Island. Reality and breath catch up to me and the magical moment is gone.

Taiamai Heritage Journeys welcomes me to these islands. I wear reef shoes and am bundled for the wind as they pair my group by height. I roll up my pant cuffs, wade across crunchy sand and slippery muck, then step aboard a *waka taua* (war canoe) to paddle up the Waitangi River. Our destination is Haruru Falls, its sheer basalt banks once used by European traders as a natural loading dock. Big man, historian, and river guide Hone Mihaka teaches about the *hoe* (paddle) and its proper use. He calls cadence from the bow in the native tongue of his Ngupuhi *iwi* (nation), a pleasing sing-song that keeps two dozen paddlers dipping in rhythm. Before long we are all singing too, and hardly notice when the *waka* runs aground on a sand bar. His grandson jumps over the side to free us, while Hone pulls a bone flute from his left earlobe and plays a haunting tune with his nose.

Back on shore, I walk the placid nature preserve paths of the treaty grounds where *Te Tiriti* (Treaty) of Waitangi, New Zealand's founding document, was signed in 1840. Low clouds trundle by and cast shifting shadows over the waters of the bay, a kaleidoscope of aquamarine, muted seafoam green, and dusty blue. Returning to Sea Princess by tender boat, I realize with sadness that the last amazing port call is now behind me.

Maybe it's not about the happy ending. Maybe it's about the story.

> I am willing to go anywhere, anywhere, anywhere;
> so long as it's forward. ~ David Livingstone

6

Nothing really prepares you for the end. The ship sees just another day, on a westerly course through the Tasman Sea, and makes hourly progress toward my final destination of Sydney. But suddenly it is all over. Things unsaid will remain unsaid. Things undone string out behind me as opportunities left untouched in the realm of possible pasts, lost forever in the flow of time. Adventurers are not programmed for stopping. But ever onward is the way of ships, and we the crew must all eventually step ashore for the last time. Every adventure must end.

It is a day of "last time ever" and "final goodbyes." The last coffee and laughs with the breakfast club. Perhaps the last battles at the laundry. The final choir practice. Fleeting final moments up on deck, bundled for the cold, watching southern ocean waves racing north. The crests flit and flee and tease my gaze to the horizon. By the time my eye catches one to focus on, it is gone. Like phantom stalkers they lurk beyond my reach, promising to guard the edge of the world for the eternity that will come once I am gone.

Things are not all glum and dour. Big smiles and hugs accompany "last" encounters with shipmates who have shared these many days during the journey around the world. We take photos together, swap addresses, and make promises to write. With deliberation I prepare my last dressy outfit and iron it with care for the last formal dinner. We finish the last bottle of prize champagne, then head off for a side-splitting comedy act and conversation.

The passenger lounge is busy and loud. Choir directors Alan and Alana wander through, join Ed and me, and share a bottle of Shiraz as thanks for our help with the summer's music. We talk and laugh until 1:00 a.m. and do not mind the hour. Many others are also up late, gathered in small groups. Excitement, for these few minutes, is strong enough to postpone tomorrow.

Daily Position: S 34º 11' 07'', E 167º 10' 01''
Status: Westerly course through the Tasman Sea
Weather: High scattered, 17º C, SE 20 kts, 3 m waves

Daily Position: S 34º 00' 00" E 157º 49' 02"
Status: Course 272º westward through the Tasman Sea
Weather: Sunny, 20º C, SE 19 kts, 3 m waves

DAY 104

TASMAN SEA

SEPTEMBER 1

Throughout this trip, I have mentioned my brain cancer infrequently but its effects are with me every single day. The cancer is like a sinister actor, always pushing me away from "absolutely!" in the direction of "maybe not today." The word 'no' is a default part of every choice, and reversing it to 'yes' requires strength and effort, each and every time.

Some decisions are beyond my control. By their nature they demand a 'yes' and require my complete attention. For example, I must step ashore tomorrow, for the last time. Only the depressing effort of packing remains. I think of Pharaohs packing for the afterlife. What stays and what goes? Choices are unavoidable. Objects hold memories, and to leave something behind means admitting any value it once had is gone. All summer has been a slow unpacking, and now it is a wild scramble to cram all this stuff into just two pieces of luggage for my next journey, onward and backward to my former life in another world.

Even amidst the chaos that colors everything on the last day at sea, our crew maintains routine. A relaxed urgency bubbles beneath a day filled with effort. I start early: breakfast with our Sydney friends, then back to the cabin for packing. Then a final lunch with new friends, and back again for more packing and more choices. I donate some old cloths to the ship for distribution to South Pacific islanders. My uneaten snacks go to friends amongst the crew: in my bag or in my belly, they will not fit. There are two dozen items not subject to any scrutiny, however: the globetrotting objects sent along by trusting sponsors. Each has completed the journey with success, and they feel like old friends. Into the bag they go.

The ship continues on a westerly course during the final hours of this epic journey around the world. Ending a glorious run, the clocks are rolled back for the 24th and final time, and with packing done I enjoy a well-earned hour of extra sleep.

We travel not to escape life, but for life not to escape us.
~ Anonymous

> *It is good to have an end to journey toward;*
> *but it is the journey that matters, in the end. ~ Ernest Hemingway*

The drama, anticipation, and tears are over. As I make preparations to leave the ship, I am blessed with a warm and rainless sky. This morning Ed and I have finished a journey around the world! We backtrack under a brilliant sunrise through Sydney harbor to the exact point from which we left, 104 nights ago. We have sailed 34,634 nautical miles, crossed 13 major bodies of water and all 360° of longitude between 62° north and 37° south latitude, to visit Australia, the Great Barrier Reef, Singapore, Malaysia, India, United Arab Emirates, Egypt, Jordan, the Suez Canal, Israel, Greece, Turkey, Anzac Cove, Italy, Vatican City, Monaco, Spain, the Straight of Gibraltar, Portugal, Ireland, Scotland, France, England, Holland, Denmark, Norway, Faroe Islands, United States of America, Aruba, Curaçao, the Panama Canal, Costa Rica, the Hawaiian Islands, American Samoa, Fiji, and New Zealand - 40 ports in 28 countries across six continents. My dream has been transformed into a sparkling collection of memories too numerous to count. Now I must start the journey home.

My closest new friends are waiting to say goodbye as we all complete paperwork to clear Australian customs. Then it is rush rush rush to get ashore, my small bags draped and shifting on their straps and big bags clunking down the gangway. As I am about to step ashore for the last time, I pause to look down at my feet. The concrete is the same, the terminal bustles with the same energy, the smells have not changed. But the instant my shoes touch this pier I will be changed forever and assume a new title: world traveler.

A throng of other passengers crowd behind me, and there is no time to savor the moment. Our replacements are on the pier, looking up at the ship and thinking the same exciting things we thought just four months ago. X sometimes marks the spot, my friends, but this I firmly believe: the world is just the start.

Daily Position: S 33º 51' 08", E 151º 12' 38"
Status: Sydney, Australia - circumnavigation completed
Weather: Clear & sunny, 25º C, SE 5 kts, calm harbor

Aboard ship the world is far, far away; it has
ceased to exist for you - seemed a fading dream,
along in the first days; has now dissolved to an
unreality; it is gone from your mind with all its
businesses and ambitions, its prosperities and
disasters, its exultations and despairs, its joys
and griefs and cares and worries. They are no
concern of yours any more; they have gone out
of your life; they are a storm which has passed
and left a deep calm behind.

~ Mark Twain in *Following the Equator.*

THE EPIC JOURNEY

WEST BY SEA

THE WORLD

AROUND

Know All Ye by These Presents, and to all polywogs, mermaids, sea serpents, whales, porpoises, sharks dolphins, eels, skates, crabs, lobsters and other living denizens of the sea. *Greetings: Know ye that*

each faithful reader of this journal

PARTICIPATED IN A JOURNEY AROUND THE WORLD AND IS COUNTED AMONG THE HONORED MEMBERS OF THE WEST BY SEA SOCIETY

EPILOGUE

After nearly four hectic but breathtaking months at sea, I returned to the world late in the year and had to face some hard realities. The house did not rent or sell, so Ed and I made the tough decision to take it off the market, have the furniture and boxes redelivered, and move back in.

That disappointment and associated extra work was just the start, as the routine check-up a month later showed my tumor had started growing again. Proton radiation had given me four stable years. Now the doctors were recommending a third craniotomy to remove the new growth. I scheduled the prodecure for January.

Postoperative tests revealed another setback: the tumor had become a more agressive Grade III anaplastic astrocytoma. Also post-surgery, I experienced significant paralysis symptoms on the left side of my body. After a quick trip to the local emergency room, a two week tapering program of steroids reduced the intracranial swelling. Still, it was a huge scare.

My lead neurooncologist checked the tumor cell pathology and crafted a six-month regimen of tailored chemotherapy. The chemo was formulated based on two monthly blood level checks, then mailed overnight and taken by mouth at home. The process greatly reduced travel back and forth to Boston. Each monthly round of chemo was more difficult to endure than the last, but my fingers were crossed.

One year after completing the circumnavigation, my exams revealed a stable tumor site, with no new growth, and therefore a reprieve from additional chemotherapy. And it was time to get back to writing.

Distance from an event provides some perspective. For a travel memoir, I think taking some time to let the experience settle in is essential. Things that seemed important in the moment, cataloged in my journal, fade in comparison to what now seem to be larger lessons. The need for distance also applies to writing. Each day we live has a beginning, middle, and end - so I tried to craft each daily page as a story-within-the-story. Looking back at a day always brings out a theme, fully hidden by events of the moment. The lesson is this: never make your first draft your last draft. Your first try always deserves a second look. There is always something hiding behind the narrative, like islands in the fog. Islands in the fog matter. Find them.

Your soul does indeed follow 24 hours behind your body. The trip was four months of new experiences, always physically in a new place one day before understanding the last place. The *meaning* of heat in India did not matter the day I tried to escape it. The *importance* of paddling a Maori canoe had no context until soreness caught up with my muscles the next day. I did not *see* the casual poverty of children in Fiji until I played back their laughter and dirty faces in my mind. There was never a day that was boring. There was never a day I didn't learn something. There was never a day when I didn't want *more*, mostly more *time*: in a port, or to watch the waves, or to spend in a slow conversation, turning strangers into friends. Time to understand. Time to savor. Time to *finish*. Just more time.

Joy in life comes from the experience of contrasts. Contrasts need two things: movement and stillness. Stillness makes a contrast *concrete*, locking each experience to a place, time, or feeling. Movement makes a contrast *possible*, pushing space between events - physical space, temporal space, emotional space. Movement and stillness together shape points along the trackline. It is important, if you care about finding any joy in life, to seek stillness as you move between experiences. This crazy journey around the world was filled with joy. Each day's experience moved me between points of stillness: while overlooking a sweeping harbor, or lost in a museum, or escaping the heat in a small cafe. Stopping to enjoy these moments was a choice, a fully intentional pause in the chaos of movement and travel and life. Perhaps this whole trip, sprinting around the planet, was really just a four-month pause in the action. I hope my adventure will inspire you to seek your own joy, on an intentional excursion beyond your own regular life. Go follow your dreams. The only goal that matters is the horizon.

ACKNOWLEDGEMENTS

Ed and I would like to thank the following individuals and groups for helping to make the West By Sea adventure possible.

First, a hearty thank you to our parents, Frances & Richard and Martha & Edward. Michelle's parents fostered LaVache during the trip and helped with logistics. Ed's parents maintained our house during the time at sea. For your advice and support, we love you Mom and Dad.

A special thank you to Princess Cruises. The Sea Princess, under Captains William Kent and Martin Stenzel, was a tight ship crewed by an absolutely magical, engaging team who provided unwaveringly positive customer service. You addressed our few concerns quickly and with competence, and graciously found ways to showcase our technology, musical, and juggling talents. We would love to return as guest lecturers, any time.

In 1999, First Command Financial Planning started a values-based plan to help realize our dreams. This book proves planning works. Special thanks to our long-time representatives Milt Salter and Robert Sampson.

We are grateful to our HGVC CruisesOnly travel representative Valerie Brissae for completing reservations, and to Delta Airlines and the Hilton family of hotels for travel and lodging to and from Australia.

A huge Yankee thank you to Merrilyn and John Corben for hosting our stay in Sydney - you are true friends who showed us the meaning of Aussie hospitality; it was great to spend the second part of the voyage with you.

Alison Downs was our exceptional lead editor. Any remaining inaccuracies, errors, or omissions are the fault of the authors. For Peter, Jan, Nancy, and Michael; thank you for working to sell our house. For Linda and Vince Ruta, thank you for adopting our rescued sister cats into a loving home. Thanks to the Naval Branch Medical Clinic in Groton for taking care of all our overseas immunizations, and Flagg RV in Uxbridge, Massachusetts for helping outfit the book tour.

Many things have inspired our yearning for travel, exploration, and adventure, but Disney's *The Adventurer's Club* holds a fond and lasting place in our memories. Please, Disney, bring it back.

Thanks to Alan and Alana Cooper for your tireless work with the underway singers; to Hutch for good friendship and excellent port knowledge, Lyn Hury for insight into the world of a guest lecturer; Ricardo Tambosi for expert insider advice, Bonie our capable cabin steward, and Tim Donovan, Matt Thompson, Kim, Martin, Mikey, Mark, and Brandon (our Alabama connection) for successfully filling the idle hours underway.

To our waiters Benjamin & Nandy, and our dining companions from Traviata table 108, first sitting, you made our time together an absolute joy each and every night. Undaunted by poor quality champagne in pursuit of daily trivia or riddle victories, we drank entirely too many free bottles and loved every minute. Thank you Maxine & Bruce, Larraine & Burt, and Karen & Roger. We will see you again soon.

Michelle would like to specifically thank and acknowledge the following people and groups.

I need to thank my parents again for always being there when I need you, no matter the distance and having been a difficult child. Thank you to my brother Peter and his wife Laurie for their support and love. To Lori B., thanks for your incredible support and friendship all these years since our early days in aviation, and making me laugh about the worst things possible. That helped me come up with, "If you can't laugh about it, you might as well be six feet under!" My Aunt Dotty always traveled during my birthday, brought me back some of the coolest gifts, and inspired my dream to travel around the world: we lost you too soon and everywhere I go you are with me. My husband, Edward for helping make those travel dreams come true and being the best travel companion. My dear friend Eric A., thank you for our mutual support since we were kids with medical issues that continue until this day and being there for each other all these years. Nean, Sueflay, and Tahn; I cannot thank you enough for your friendship through the years, after Peter dubbed us "the Fantastic Four." Kathi and David Callahan, true Coast Guard friends through and through. Thank you both for being there to help after my first craniotomy. And to all the spouses in the CG Spouses Association of Mobile, Alabama who came by with meals after my surgery, I cannot tell you enough how much that helped! Lisa, Bryan, Traci, and Chris, thank you for your amazing friendship and support while we lived in Mobile and to this day.

And a huge thanks to some very special people who are no longer with us who motivate me to keep fighting to live. Especially Nicole Branch-Bickman who always said "I live to confound" because she kept living despite doctors and nurses giving up on her! During our last phone call before Nicole passed, I told her I would "see her soon" and she said to me, "Not too soon!" So I promised to keep fighting. My dear friend Heather Bush who was my Southern Etiquette Checker: we did good work together your last day here on this planet entertaining children with cancer at Camp Rap-a-hope during their last day of their "Searching for Camelot" program. And many other Brain Cancer Warriors who are now angels that inspire me daily to keep up the warrior attitude even when things get worse, such as Nikki Perry, David Welsh, and so many others: you inspire me each day I wake up and am thankful I can function and not be too much of a burden. And to all I call family and friends (your names would take many pages), thank you for your support every day that helps get us through this challenging journey.

Attitude is one part of the Cancer Warrior's daily life, a second part is having great support from family and friends, and a third is caring doctors. My surgeons and doctors were a huge part of that and I never had the same one twice due to moving in the military. Dr. Edward Flotte of Coastal Neurological Institute in Mobile, Alabama, thank you for saving my life! Dr. Martin Holland, along with Dr. Wayne Gluf and the team at the Naval Medical Center, San Diego for giving me more time with a debulking surgery. I am now seen at Massachusetts General Hospital in Boston. The doctors I have at MGH are fantastic and help keep me going. Dr. Helen Shih, my radiation oncologist, I am thrilled to have been part of your clinical trial for low-grade glioma treatment with Proton Radiation, which gave me four additional years of good life and allowed me to take this amazing journey. I hope others will benefit from this treatment.

Thank you to the team at the Dr. Francis Burr Proton Radiation Center for making this happen: Mary Ellen, Georgene, Allisha, Hui, John, Phil, Carmen, and of course Paul at the front desk. My endocrinologist Dr. Nicolas Tritos treats me for the after effects of radiation. I also need to thank Dr. William Curry for performing my third craniotomy after the cancer grew back. Thanks to my neurooncologist Dr. Elizabeth Gerstner for putting me on chemo to tame the new, nastier beast.

A special thanks to our friends in North Square, Boston; CAPT Michael Cicclese and the fantastic team at the Mariner's House; and Linda Riccio, Chef Marisa Iocco, and the exceptional staff at Gennaro's.

One last huge thanks to my doctors and nurses at the Naval Health Clinic in Groton. Especially to Elise Roy and Coleen Miller: I would never have made it to Boston without all of your help getting endless referrals for many years. Every day is a little victory and I could not have done it without all of you (ten years and counting), thank you.

Edward would like to specifically thank the following people.

First, thanks again to my mom and dad. If anybody needs an example of model parents, you are at the top of the list. Keep traveling!

My aunts and uncles have always pushed me towards adventure with trips, stories, books, or by example. Mom's siblings Sharon, Allan, Peter, Carol, and Floyd, and dad's brothers Roger, Duane, Alan, and Greg: thank you all for your kind support and tough love when I needed it. The same goes for your spouses Richard, Janice, Linda, Irene, Janet, and Anne.

My early mentor and friend, Sean McCarthy succumbed to aggressive brain cancer in 2009. I regret not making time to walk with him across the Brooklyn Bridge. He drilled speed, accuracy, and quality in all things, and set me loose on my first treasure hunt, Kit Williams' *Masquerade*. I will carry the memory of his bright-eyed questioning all my days.

Thank you to Lavinia Spalding and Rolf Potts for an intense travel writing workshop at the Riverlight Center in Mystic, Connecticut. Your advice helped fill many gaps that saved me trouble later. I raise a full glass of Arizona wine to Gayle and Eric Glomski for showing by your inspiring example the power of following dreams in the face of adversity.

Navigational archaeologist and friend Rick Gay helped craft a top-notch treasure hunt, vetted by my longtime friend and cipher expert Charles Gray. Ben Boyer painted the circumnavigation certificate. My friend Bill Parry has been an unwavering champion throughout the project.

Special thanks to my brothers: Andrew who proofed text and was state-side webmeister during the journey, and William at 1410 Media for audio, video, and photographic support. Don't get no security involved.

And finally, my strongest possible thanks to Michelle, my amazing wife, for keeping up the fight. You are the perfect traveling companion: curious, capable, and beautiful. I look forward to many amazing journeys together!

We must highlight and thank the 153 Kickstarter backers who paid for the underway blog, multimedia technology and software, and journaling equipment - and to DJ Grandpa's podcast, Sports Car Junkie Business podcast, New London Patch, and JetSet Times for sharing the story. You stuck with us through the entire trip and an extra year battling cancer. You have to give to get. This book is proof that dreams, with a team, can indeed come true. Thank you all.

KICKSTARTER BACKERS

No reward requested

Abdullah Rufus	Fernando Macias-Jimenez
Clayton Hanson	Joanne French
Dave Ranta	Kathleen Borsos-Wooley
Frances & Richard Boullianne	Kathleen Liles

Segment Backers
Please visit the links for and patronize each of these five generous backers

Segment 1: JD Henning	*Keys of Electrum*	tinyurl.com/keysofelectrum
Segment 2: Andrew Milham	*Zeode Software Design*	zeode.com
Segment 3: edward laing	*pzizz technology limited*	pzizz.com
Segment 4: Bram Britcher	*Brittmore Group LLC*	brittmore.com
Segment 5: Don Trone	*Leadership Center for Investment Stewards*	3ethos.com

Bookbinder Backers

Wayne & Christina Johnson	Geoffrey Paul	Thomas A. Kinney
Tom and Dottie Matteson		Joseph Cardin

Vagabonder Backer

Ron Foerch

Voyager Backers
For these backers we carried a small object around the world

Jackie Leverich
Pete & Laurie
Mike and Laura Sundquist
Anne, Claire and Catherine Fitzgerald
Matt
Nancy and Ty Thill
Willington Beales
Martha and Ed Beale
Erica Mohr
juicies.com

Toni, Rick and Brendan Gay
Bill Wertz
Bill Parry
Duane and Janet Beale
Connie
Kathy R
South Berwick Beales
Alo Konsen
Claudia Ribeiro

Wanderer Backers

Robert DeCoopman
Matt & Julia Baker
Lori Butler
Mark Dietrich
Pady
SS FRG ATCT

Scott & Marion Gesele CGA '92
Schenk Schenk
Fr Thomas Weise CGA '92
The Wilson Family - All 10 of us.
Michael B Cooper
Joe & LaRae Malinauskas

Adventurer Backers

Elmar Henne
Dan McLaughlin
Christopher Harrison
Sigrid
Rick Cehon

Margaret L. Brown
Jamie Smith
Mark Bryant
Ralph

Expeditionnaire Backers

Michael P. Chien
Jenn & Jim Canfield
Charlie Coiro
Anonymous
Jeff Marsick
Linda Palmer
James Young
Mark & Elizabeth Markley

Big Z
David Walter
Jonathan Heller
Nancy and Jack Almeida
Kristen Serumgard
John W. Pruitt, III
Chris Conway

Journaler Backers

Katie Hood, Camden, NC
Cadman Family
Mary Sheahan
Eleanor Ali
Lebanon Palmers
Mary Kaye
Patricia Charles
Jason Warren
Olna Jenn Smith
Rob & Deb Sherwood

Will Ciaburri
Sidonie Sansom
Bob & Ann Kaylor
Allison Rossett
Jim Miller
Chris & Diana Kent
Mary Hagerman
Jim Marshall
The Kamphausen Family
Charlie & Cathy (Kircher) Hyde & Family

The Smith Family - Deane, Melissa, Thad, Nate, & Zane

eJournaler Backers

Danielle Romano
Al Hoefer
My Favorite Swimmer Ever
Dennis Callahan
Marc Matoba
David J. Obedzinski
Carolyn Wolfram
Casey and Tiffany Jones

Cousin Adie
Jesse Franks
Mike Metzler
Norman Picard
Bob & SaraBeth Nivison
Dina Hannigan
Leslie Berry
Theresa Palmer

Cliff Their
Peter Leeds
captain_turk
Jenna Tucker
Kathy Ruby
Joe Staier
Cate Griffin
Phil Prather

Steve Vigus from Sports Car Junkies Business Podcast   Kapil Chandra
Thank YOU for the journey - Melissa   Philip F. Kordon & Jessica L. Kordon

Card Club Backers

Igor Klimer	Ian Thorpe	Christy Newell
Dan Silvers	Hugh Griffin	Paige
Carmen Rose Shenk	George Antonakos	Jacqueline Boone
Adriana Atencio	Christopher Berinato	Adam Farnsworth
Christine Koenig Mclaughlin	Donna Dominick	Mirko Klopfleisch
Mary Hagerman	Tim Sullivan	Robert Linder
Dawn Sherman Meisner	J. LeBlanc	Michelle & Joe Bezzina
Laura Evangelista	Alexander Hawson	Corbin Lorick

Bandwidth Backers

Matthew Martin	Christopher Theodore	Kathy Moss Torrez
Deivis Slavinskas	Justin P. Moore	

4-44-80-48-53-96-44-12-60-12-37-42-18-12

75-101-63-34-44-15-34-18-12-78-15-44-34-9-40-18-37-76-37-80-12-88-60

31-96-28-60-66-56-91-12-60-56-60-101-12-12-48-42-12

TREASURE HUNT

This book contains an armchair treasure hunt. Locate and decipher multi-layered clues spread across one hundred and five daily logbook pages, to reveal a geographic position *and* a final offset clue, that together pinpoint a specific physical spot on the surface of planet Earth.

Solving the layered puzzle will require only paper and pencil, the ability to read and understand the English language, a keen eye for detail, creativity, and tenacity. If you uncover the final position and offset clue, contact us with your answer. An independent committee will review each submission, and assign recognition for those found to be correct. If correct, we will add your name to a publicly displayed honor roll. We do not influence committee decisions. Committee decisions are final.

If you choose to actually travel to the final location, **bring paper and crayon to make a rubbing** of the *correct* object. Hint: the position revealed by this book will only get you close. You must also decode and use the offset to locate the final object. The first ten (10) people to send us a rubbing, and subsequently solve a final question based on the book codes (thereby proving you visited the final spot *and* have also cracked the underlying book code), will receive a limited-edition object, and 1% of the book profits for the remainder of the first five (5) years of publication.

Keep in mind, this is not a contest or a drawing, but a treasure hunt.

This means if you choose to participate, you assume responsibility for any and all expenses, and take all risks as a private individual. There are no prizes or awards other than those already outlined above.

Some notes about the site: it is outdoors and wheelchair accessible during normal daytime hours, and under video surveillance. There is nothing buried under the object, so do not dig it up. Just make a quick rubbing, and enjoy the view. **Adhere to all local regulations getting to and from the site, and leave everything as you found it.**

Treasure hunters who are confident in their solution must contact us by email, replacing *YYYY* with 2016, 2017, 2018, 2019 or 2020 depending on the current year: *treasureYYYY@westbysea.com.* The email date and time adjusted for GMT, or postmark date if applicable, will set precedence of solutions. We will provide additional instructions and a mailing address, if warranted by your submission.

After 31 December 2020, the decoder keys will be published, and after that date 100% of every sale benefits charity.

Happy hunting.

Some media from the journey may be licensed for royalty-free use. Visit www.westbysea.com for more information.

Proceeds from this book,
after expenses and treasure awards, if any,
are donated directly to charities on a quarterly basis,
with the intent to benefit
brain cancer treatment and research,
ovarian cancer research,
families of deployed military personnel,
and wounded veterans.

Thank you for sharing our story. Now go write your own.

ABOUT THE AUTHORS

Michelle M. B. Beale is a native of Bethpage, New York, USA, home of Grumman and the F-14 Tomcat. A life-long aviation enthusiast, she completed a dual bachelors degree in Aeronautics and Management. She worked at the Port Authority of New York and New Jersey in Tower One of New York City's World Trade Center; Newark, John F. Kennedy and LaGuardia airports; Operations Supervisor and Noise Abatement Officer for KFRG Republic Airport; and Program Manager for the U. S. Coast Guard Academy's Institute for Leadership. Michelle was diagnosed with brain cancer in early 2006 and has battled through three craniotomies, experimental proton radiation, and chemotherapy to bring this tale to you.

Edward K. Beale is a native of Tolland, Connecticut, USA. At an early age Ed fell in love with puzzles, codes, ciphers and travel, and set out to unlock the world. He has since visited 50 states, 49 countries, and all seven continents. He retired from the United States Coast Guard after two decades of service as a shipboard deck watch officer, rescue helicopter pilot, polar science operations senior aviator, and dean of students, curricula, and instructors at the USCG Leadership Development Center. He speaks regularly at learning & performance conferences, and actively promotes positive organizational culture and strategic leadership.

This is their first book written together, but probably not the last.

Life is not a race,
but a journey to be savored
each step of the way.
Yesterday is history,
tomorrow is a mystery,
but today is a gift.